AF540453

Aquaculture

NIPA® GENX ELECTRONIC RESOURCES & SOLUTIONS P. LTD.
New Delhi-110 034

About the Author

Dr. Sudhan Chandran is working at Fisheries College and Research Institute, Tamil Nadu. Dr. J. Jayalalithaa Fisheries University, as Assistant Professor in Department of Fisheries Biology and Resource Management. He is teaching Fisheries Biology and Resource Management related course for under graduate students. He is a recipient of ICAR-CIFE fellowship for Doctor of Philosophy in Fisheries Resource Management at ICAR-Central Institute of Fisheries Education, Mumbai. To his credit, he published several research papers in national and international journals including 5 years of experience in research and 3 years in teaching programmes.

Aquaculture Points to Remember

Sudhan C.
Fisheries College and Research Institute
(Tamil Nadu Dr. J. Jayalalithaa Fisheries University)
Thoothukudi, Tamil Nadu, India

NIPA® GENX ELECTRONIC RESOURCES & SOLUTIONS P. LTD.
New Delhi-110 034

NIPA® GENX ELECTRONIC RESOURCES & SOLUTIONS P. LTD.

101,103, Vikas Surya Plaza, CU Block
L.S.C. Market, Pitam Pura, New Delhi-110 034
Ph : +91-11-43860225, Mob.: +91 9717133558, 9540816132
E-mail: newindiapublishingagency@gmail.com
Website: www.nipaersources.com

Print ISBN: 978-93-58873-56-6

eISBN: 978-93-58878-44-8

Composed and Designed by NIPA®.

Preface

Aquaculture and fisheries sciences have emerged as dynamic and essential disciplines in the face of rising global demand for sustainable food sources, nutrition security, and rural livelihoods. The present volume, structured to comprehensively cover the major domains of aquaculture, aquatic environment, fish processing, engineering, health management, and biotechnology, is designed to cater to the academic and practical needs of undergraduate and postgraduate students, researchers, professionals, and policy planners involved in the aquatic sector. The book is divided into well-defined thematic sections that reflect the multidisciplinary nature of the field. It begins with foundational principles of aquaculture, including freshwater systems, ornamental fishery practices, hatchery management, and feed technology. Subsequent sections delve into fish taxonomy, anatomy, physiology, and stock assessment, which are fundamental to resource management.

The aquatic environment is explored through the lenses of limnology, climatology, and pollution, setting the ecological context for aquatic life. Fish health and pathology, a critical area for disease prevention and control, are given due emphasis. A dedicated portion of the book discusses modern fish processing techniques, value addition, microbiology, and quality assurance—highlighting the importance of post-harvest technology and food safety.

Another core section focuses on fisheries engineering, covering aquaculture infrastructure, fishing gear, navigation, and marine instrumentation. Extension education, disaster preparedness, project management, and marketing aspects bring in the socio-economic dimension, ensuring the holistic development of the sector.

Finally, the book introduces emerging frontiers in fish biotechnology and genetics, underscoring their potential to revolutionize aquaculture productivity and resilience.

This book is the outcome of combined efforts by subject experts and practitioners who have synthesized their knowledge into concise, curriculum-aligned chapters enriched with scientific insights and real-world applications.

We hope this compilation will serve as a valuable resource for learners, educators, and professionals aiming to contribute to the sustainable growth of the fisheries and aquaculture industry.

We extend our sincere gratitude to all contributors, reviewers, and institutions whose support made this work possible.

Editors

Contents

Fish Processing Technology

Fisheries Engineering and Post Harvest Management

Fisheries Extension, Economics and Statistics

Fisheries Genetics and Biotechnology

Aquaculture

1

Principles of Aquaculture

1. Alkalinity is expressed as equivalents of **calcium carbonate**.
2. Adult fish retained for spawning is called as **brood stock**.
3. The population, number or weight of a species that is present in that environment is called as **carrying capacity**.
4. The discharge from a rearing facility, treatment plant or industry is called as **effluent**.
5. The ability of water to neutralize soap is due to presence of **cations (calcium and magnesium)**.
6. Very soft water – **0 to 20 ppm as $CaCO_3$**.
7. Soft water – **21 to 50 ppm as $CaCO_3$**.
8. Hard water – **51 to 500 ppm as $CaCO_3$**.
9. Very hard water – **above 500 ppm as $CaCO_3$**.
10. Aquaculture is believed to be first practices as early as 2000 B.C. in **China**.
11. China is called as **"Cradle of aquaculture"**.
12. "THE CLASSIC OF FISH CULTURE" – written by **Fan Lai**.
13. King Someswara son of **King Vikramaditya VI** was first to record the common sport fishes of India.
14. **AICRP** – All India Coordinated Research Project.
15. **IARI** – Indian Agricultural Research Institute.
16. Early fingerlings – **35 to 50 mm**.
17. Advanced fingerlings – **80 to 100 mm** (10 to 15 cm).
18. Juveniles – **150 mm**.
19. Size of Hapa net – **2 x 1 x 1 m**.
20. Size of Transportation bag is **84 x 61 cm**.
21. Thickness of transportation bag is **0.6 mm**.
22. **Acclimatization** is the process of adjustment of two different environmental conditions.

23. Fringed lipped carp – ***Labeo fimbriatus***.
24. Pig mouth carp – ***Labeo kontius***.
25. Bata – ***Labeo bata***.
26. White carp – ***Cirrhinus cirrhosa***.
27. Reba – ***Cirrhinus reba***.
28. Fresh water shark – ***Wallago attu***.
29. Giant freshwater prawn –***Macrobrachium rosenbergii***.
30. Cauvery prawn – ***M. malcolmsonii***.
31. Tiger shrimp – ***Penaeus monodon***.
32. Indian white shrimp – ***Penaeus indicus***.
33. American white shrimp – ***Litopenaeus vannamei***.
34. Sea bass – ***Lates calcarifer***.
35. Milk fish – ***Chanos chanos***.
36. Pearl spot – ***Etroplus suratensis*** (green chromidae).
37. Pearl spot – ***E. maculatus*** (orange chromidae).
38. Mud crab – ***Scylla serrate*** (cultured variety).
39. Mud crab – ***S. tranquibarica*** (commonly found in the waters).
40. INDOCERT – **Indian Organic Certification**.
41. NPOP – **National programme for Organic Production**.
42. USDA – **United States Department of Agriculture**.
43. Optimum level of alkalinity **40-150 ppm**.
44. Soft water contain hardness about **less than 40 ppm**.
45. **1 ppm** lime can reduce **0.9 ppm of** CO_2.
46. Optimum limit of ammonia **0.3 - 1.3 ppm**.
47. Optimum level of nitrite **3.5 ppm**.
48. Hydrogen sulphides should be below **0.05 ppm**.
49. Transparency should be **20-40 cm**.
50. 0ptimum **PH 6.5-8.5**.
51. Nursery pond also called as **transplantation pond**.
52. Nursery pond culture days **15 - 30 days**.
53. Hormone weedicide **-2, 4, - D & 2, 4, 5, T**.
54. **Copper sulphate** used to remove the algal bloom.
55. Water stick insect – **Ranatra**.

56. Giant water bugs – **belostoma**.
57. Water seorpion – **laccotrephes**.
58. Back swimmer – **Anisops**.
59. Dragon fly nymphs are highly predatory on **carp spawn**.
60. Soap oil emulsion prepared by mixing of **soap & oil at the ratio of 1:3**.
61. Commercial detergent – **Teepol B -306**.
62. The chinese are world leader for the **culture of freshwater pearl**.
63. Pearl is the **biological germ**.
64. **Pearl** is born of love-hate relationship.
65. Guppy introduced from **South America at 1908**.
66. *Gambusia affinis* introduced from **Italy at 1928**.
67. Red piranha- ***serrasalmus nattereri***.

2

Freshwater Aquaculture

1. A production of 600 tones/ha/year of tilapia in cages has been recorded in **Laguna Bay in Philippines**.
2. Indian Major Carps (IMC) contributes **84%** of India's aquaculture production.
3. The seed production of the carps has been standardized, with commercial hatcheries producing over **19000 million** fry per year.
4. A pit like structure located near the outlet of the pond is called as **harvesting pit (measures about 50 - 100m^2)**.
5. Size of the nursery pond = **12 x 6 x 1m**.
6. Size of the Rearing pond = **25 x 12 x 1m**.
7. Size of the production pond is **0.1 to 2 ha**.
8. Size of the quarantine pond is less than **0.5 ha**.
9. During construction to retard erosion and seepage, soil must contain a minimum of **25% of clay**.
10. The depth of the pond must be **0.5 to 1m**.
11. Sufficient water should be available to provide **100 to 250 l/ min/ ha** of total pond area.
12. Average plankton production per m^3 should range between **10 ml and 20 ml**.
13. Organophosphates used in India are **DDVP, Phosphamidon, thiomatin** *etc*.
14. Dose rate of organophoaphates are **3 to 30 ppm**.
15. In Assam, ***Milletia piscida*** and ***Milletia pachycarpra*** are used to eradicate unwanted fishes.
16. Tea seed cake – ***Camellia sasargua, C. semiserrata***.
17. Calcium hypochlorite is also called as **bleaching powder**.
18. Bleaching powder contains **30% of chlorine**.
19. Turpentine is applied at the rate of **250 litre/ ha** is applied for eradication of unwanted fishes.

20. Saponin – a **hemolytic toxin**.
21. Out of 11 orders of class Insecta, 3 orders namely.
    a. Hemiptera (Water Bugs)
    b. Coleoptera (Water Beetles)
    c. Odonata (Flies) are relatively more common in fresh water ponds
22. Hemiptera
    a. Lithocerus – Giant Water Bug
    b. Nepa – Water Scorpion
    c. Ranatra – Water Stick Insect
    d. Notonecta – Back Swimmers
    e. Geirs – Water Spider
23. Coleopteran
    a. Cybister – Water Beetles
    b. Dytiscus – Diving Beetles
    c. Hydrophilus – Scavenger Beetles
    d. Gyrinus – Whirling Beetles
24. Odonata
    a. Dragon fly
    b. Damsel fly
25. Mustard oil or coconut oil along with cheap washing soap at the ratio of **56:18 kg/ ha** is a well-known technique developed by **CIFRI** for control of predatory insects within few hours of its application.
26. The oil of **Alexandrium laurel** and Water dispersible gammexane commonly known as **Hertex** U.P. are effective to kill insects.
27. SSP – **Single Super Phosphate (16 - 20% - commercial form)**.
28. TSP – **Triple Super Phosphate (40 - 45% - commercial form)**.
29. The maximum ammonia concentration permitted for fish farming is **0.1 mg/ l**.
30. In highly alkaline soils of **8.5 to 9.5 pH** lime application is not required.
31. The standard combination of **N: P: K as 8:4:1** is commonly used to fertilize the pond.
32. **"Crips"** means pond water is fertile but not turbid.
33. Traditional way of seed transport – **Earthen pots**.
34. **Metal containers** made up of Aluminium, Galvanized iron and tin are mainly used.
35. Best anesthetic – **Carbonic acid**.

36. The **sewage** serves as a **breeding ground** for mosquitoes and other disease-causing organisms.
37. The water content of the domestic sewage is about **99 %**.
38. Floating cages have been identified since from the end of 19th century in Great Lake region of **Kampuchea**.
39. First Modern cage fish farming originated in **Japan**.
40. **Cage structure** and **Cage size** are the two main components of cage design.
41. **Round cages** are more efficiently used for schooling fishes *i.e.* **Milk fish**.
42. **Floating cage** – most widely used cage.
43. Method of erection of pens is two types namely: **Dry ground** and **wet ground**.
44. 1 ton of poultry manure as equivalent to **7 tons of farm yard manure**.
45. **Cow dung** is a main source of farm yard manure.
46. Green manures (**sun hemp – *Sesbania*** sp.).
47. Bio-herbicides – Microbial plant pathogens (which are sprayed to kill or suppress the growth of weeds).
48. Azolla – FIX nitrogen up to **100 - 150 kg/ ha**.
49. Fresh water pearl of superior quality were first produced in **Japan**, especially from its fresh water Lake **Biwa**.
50. Pearl is called as **biological gem**.
51. The **layer orientation** and **composition of aragonite** crystals layers in nacreous pearls give the **quality of the gem**.
52. Pearl has 4.0 **hardness of Moh's scale** with a specific gravity of **2.7**.
53. The graft tissue – **mantle epithelium** (2 - 3 cm^2).
54. **Round culture pearls** are obtained by gonadal implantation **surgery method**.
55. Formation of pearl through **non-nucleated** method takes about **1.2 to 2 years**.
56. Formation of pearl through **nucleated** method takes about **1 year**.
57. Fresh water prawns are **omnivorous**.
58. Pond visibility should be maintained in the range of **30 - 40 cm** to avoid water quality deterioration.
59. **Ants** are considered as the best feed for **larva of gourami**.
60. Siamese gourami is also called as **snake-skin gourami / sepat gourami**.

61. The maximum size of climbing perch recorded is **26 cm**.
62. *Anabas testudineus* – **hardy fish, omnivorous in nature**.
63. Common carp – **omnivorous in nature**.
64. In Indonesia, spawning mats made of fibres of indjuk (*Arenga* sp.) called as **Kakabans**.
65. The stickiness of the eggs of common carps are removed by **sodium carbonate and carbamide** (40 g sodium carbonate and 30 g carbamide dissolved in 10 litres of water).
66. Tawes – **Puntius javanicus**.
67. The market demand of common carp is about **500g**.
68. Rainbow trout – ***Salmo gairdneri gairdneri (Oncorynchus mykiss)***.
69. Brown trout – ***Salmo truta fario***.
70. Brook trout – ***Salvelinus fontinalis***.
71. Indian trout – ***Barilious bola***.
72. Deep bodied mahseer – ***Tor tor***.
73. Mosalmahseer – ***Tor mosal***.
74. Golden mahseer – ***Tor putitora***.
75. Atlantic salmon – ***Salmo solar***.
76. Sockeye salmon – ***Onchorynchus nerka***.
77. Coho salmon – ***Onchorynchus teisuthu***.
78. Chum or Dog salmon – ***Onchorynchus keta***.
79. Pink or humpback salmon – ***Onchorynchus gorbuscha***.
80. Pacific salmon or King salmon – ***Onchorhyncus tshawytscha***.
81. Brown trout is indigenous to **Central and Western Europe**.
82. Brook trout is native to **North Eastern North America**.
83. Eyed stage ova is observed in **trout**.
84. **King salmon** is the largest species growing up to **45 kg in weight**.
85. Coho salmon is a **hardy species**.
86. Chum or dog salmon is native to **east and west Pacific**.
87. **Pacific salmon** die after spawning.
88. Salmon fry can be reared in high densities of **10000 fry/ m^2**.
89. The **smoltification** of salmon takes place in **spring** when it undergoes physiological pre-adaptation for life in sea water.
90. The minimum size of **smolt is 15g**.

91. The maximum size of **smolt is 20 - 30g.**
92. The most common method of culturing salmon to market size is **floating sea cages** or **pens.**
93. Asian catfish – ***Clarius batrachus.***
    a. Females build nest
    b. Males take care of the eggs after spawning
    c. The nest is in the form of round holes measuring about 20 cm in diameter and 25 cm in depth.
94. Singhi – ***Heteropneustes fossilis*** (stinging catfish).
95. The maximum size of singhi recorded is **38cm.**
96. In singhi, males are smaller than **females.**
97. American catfish – ***Ictalurus punctatus.***
98. Tilapia belongs to **Cichlidae** family and native of **Africa.**
99. Jhingran and Gopalakrishnan (1974) listed **22 species** that have been used in experimental or production scale fish culture.
100. Tilapia – **mouth brooder** which incubate the fertilized eggs in the mouth of female.
101. Under tilapia new genus found to be ***Sarotherodon*** (meaning brush-toothed).
102. Species like ***Tilapia mossambica*** and ***Tilapia zillii*** can grow even in hypersaline waters of 42 ppt salinity.
103. Tilapias are mostly **herbivorous** or **omnivorous** in nature.
104. **Male** tilapia grows faster than **female** tilapia.
105. Under favorable conditions tilapia grows **500 to 800g.**
106. Total ammonia = **ionized ammonia + unionized ammonia.**
107. **Alkalinity** is defined as the **total amount of acid** required to **titrate** the bases in a water sample.
108. **Hardness** is defined as the **total soluble calcium and magnesium** salts present in the water medium, expressed as its equivalent $CaCO_3$.
109. Monsoon river prawn – ***Macrobrachium malconsoni.***
110. Orana river prawn – ***Macrobrachium idea.***
111. Giant river prawn – ***Macrobrachium rosenbergii.***

3

Ornamental Fish Production and Management

1. Ornamental fishes are also called as **living jewels**.
2. The ancient Romans were the first to keep ornamental fishes as **pets** at homes.
3. Aquarium fish can fetch **100 times** more price than the food fish.
4. Marine ornamentals fetches **10 times** more costly **than** freshwater ornamental fishes.
5. Ornamental fish farming is a boon to India for rapid development of **national economy**.
6. Values of international trade of ornamental fishes are about US $ 5 Billion.
7. Major traders of ornamental fishes are USA, Europe, Japan, Australia, Singapore, Indonesia, Philippines and Sri Lanka. **(8 countries, code word: SIPS-JEUA)**
8. The markets for ornamental fishes consist:
   a. 99% home hobbyists.
   b. 1% public aquarium and Research Institutions.
9. Estimated annual value of world trade in ornamental fishes are
   a. **US $ 1 Billion** – for Wholesale business.
   b. **US $ 1.5 Billion** – for Retail business.
10. **50%** of the suppliers of ornamental fishes were located in Asian countries.
    a. 80% - from pond raised freshwater fishes.
    b. 15% - from marine wild caught fish.
    c. 5% - fresh and brackish water wild caught fish.
11. The Major suppliers of fresh water fishes are Singapore, Thailand, Hong Kong, Japan and Malaysia. (5 countries, code word: **JaMaS - TH)**

12. The major suppliers of wild caught marine fishes are Philippines, Indonesia and Sri Lanka. (3 countries, code word: **SIP**).
13. Ornamental fish tank is also called as **Aquarium**.
14. Hood is also called as **tank cover** (made up of wood, glass or tin plate).
15. The self contained units with a container for media and an electric pump to circulate water are present in **Canister filter**.
16. **Sponge or wool** material is kept inside the poly foam filter for filtering the waste.
17. **OTP** – Overhead Trickle Purification System.
18. The filter with activated charcoal is called as **carbon filter**.
19. Gravel size fit for aquarium is **3-5mm**.
20. Surface area required for the fishes are
    a. **30 cm^2** for tropical freshwater species,
    b. 75 cm^2 for **cold freshwater species**.
21. Gold fish – ***Carassius auratus***.
22. Rosy barb – ***Barbus conchonius*** (no barbel, slight lateral compression).
23. Tiger barb – ***Barbus tetrazona*** (no barbel, 4 transverse bands, also called as **Sumatra barb**).
24. Silver shark – ***Balantiocheilus melanopterus*** (also called as **Bala shark**, Tricolor shark which has dominated eye on head).
25. Red Tailed black shark – ***Labeo bicolor*** (2 pairs of barbels).
26. Zebra Danio – ***Brachydanio rerio*** (up turned mouth).
27. Rasbora – ***Rasbora heteromorphy*** (also called as **Harlequin** fish which has long caudal peduncle with violet iridescence).
28. Cardinal tetra – ***Paracheirodon axelrodi*** (presence of green colored stripe with red band which extends the whole body length.
29. Neon tetra – ***paracheirodon innesi***.
30. Siamese fighter fish – ***Beta splendens*** (long, flowing/ cropped fins).
31. Dwarf gourami – ***Colisa lalia***.
32. Three spot gourami – ***Tricogaster trichopterus***.
33. Kissing gourami – ***Heleostoma temmincki***.
34. Discus – ***Symphysodon sp***. (also called as **Pompadour fish**).
35. Angelfish – ***Pterophyllum scalare*** (**fan** shaped caudal fin).
36. Oscar – ***Astronotus ocellatus***.

37. Firemouth cichlid – ***Cichlasoma (Thorichthys) meeki***.
38. Malawi Golden Cichlid – ***Melanochromis auratus*** (also called as Auratus).
39. Asian Arowana – ***Scleropages formosus***.
40. Guppy – ***Poecilia reticulata***.
41. Sail fin molly – ***Poecilia latipinna***.
42. Marble molly – ***Poecilia sphenops***.
43. Molly must be kept in **salt environment** (so a teaspoon of epsum salt + 5 drops of methylene blue is added to each 5 l of water).
44. Sword tail – ***Xiphophorus helleri***.
45. Platy – ***Xiphophorus maculatus***.
46. In live bearers mature male has **gonopodium**.
47. Gestation period of live bearers are being constant for every species (3-4 weeks.)
    a. Guppy – **4 - 6 week**
    b. Platy – **3 - 4 week**
    c. Molly – **5 - 7 week**
    d. Sword tail – **4 - 6 week**
48. Number of young ones expected in live bearers are
    a. On average – **40 to 60**
    b. Guppy – **100**
    c. Platy – **50**
    d. Molly – **100**
    e. Sword tail – **200**
49. Example for egg burriers – **Killifish**.
50. Examples for egg scatterers are – **Gold fish and koi carp**.
51. Examples for egg depositors – **Angel fish and Discus**.
52. Target fish can be used be help strengthen the bond between a fish pair.
53. Amazon sword plant – ***Cryptocoryne***.
54. **Red tailed black sharks** are difficult to breed because of their aggressive in nature towards their own species.
55. **Cabomba**– Washington plant / Fanwort/ water shield.
56. Egeria – Anacharis, Elodea, Ditch moss, **Canadian pond weed**.

57. Myriophyllum – Water milfoil, **foxtail**.
58. Vallisneria – **Eel grass**, tape grass, ribbon grass, corkscrew.
59. Sagittaria – **Arrow head, arrow weed**.
60. Certopterus – **Water sprite, Indian fern**.
61. Hydrophila – **Nomaphila**.
62. Microsorium – **Java fern**.
63. Cryptcoryne – Crypt, **great centerpiece plants**.
64. Echniodorous – **Sword-plants, Amazons**.
65. Aponogeton – **Madagascar lace plant**.
66. Lemna – **Duck weed**.
67. *Eleocharisa cicularis* – **Hair grass, needle grass**.
68. Some species of snails are causing a serious menace to plants. They are listed as follows,
    a. Apple snail – ***Ampullaria cuprina***.
    b. Ramshorn snail – ***Planorbis corneus***.
    c. Malayan snail – ***Melania tubercilata***.
69. The synthetically produced pigment which is most commonly used as additive is called as **Astaxanthin**.
70. **Beef heart** has been traditionally used as an effective **binder** in farm based feeds.
71. Amount of feed given per day – Biomass X % of the body weight of feed per day.
72. Biomass = Stocking density X survival X average body weight.
73. Cladocerans – **Water flea** (ranges from 0.5-1.5).
74. **Tiger bard and rosy barbdo** does not show maturation above 120 ppm water hardness.
75. Successful spawning of gold fish has been reported at **700 ppm water hardness**.
76. **Free CO_2** at a concentration of **more than** 15 ppm is detrimental to **ornamental fishes**.
77. **Koi** is known to tolerable wide variations in temperature (i.e. between 20 and 30 °C).
78. **Sword tails** are very sensitive to **25 - 27 °C**.
79. Spawning of goldfish has been successful in **24 - 26 °C**.

80. **Lymphocyctis** – a viral disease (denoted by nodular white swellings looks like cauliflower on the fins or body).
81. Mouth fungus – ***Chondrococcus columnaris***.
82. Bloating of body & protruding of scales are the typical characters of **Dropsy**.
83. Transquilizers like **quinaldine** or **paraldehyde** can be used in mild concentration to reduce the activity of fishes.
84. Common anesthetics used in fish transport:
    a. **MS - 222** (Triacaine methane sulphonate)
    b. **Quinaldine** (2 - Methyl quinaldine)
85. Risks are the part of **agribusiness**.

4

Finfish Hatchery Management

1. 21723 living species of fishes existing in the world at present.
2. **Jhingran and Gopalakrishnan** 1974 listed 314 species of teleost utilized for aquaculture throughout the world.
3. **Gynogenetic** offsprings are always **females**.
4. Bisexual fishes – **Gonochorism fishes**.
5. Protoandrous hermaphrodites – ***Lates calcarifer, Sparus auratus, Sargus sargus and Palleus mormyrus***.
6. Protogynous hermaphrodites – **groupers**.
7. **Dwarf males** were observed in **Angler fish** and **Salmonids**.
8. Sand spawners / Psammophils – ***Gobio gobio***.
9. Rock and gravel spawners – **Rohu, salmonids**.
10. Terrestrial spawners / aerophils – ***Bryconpetrosus***.
11. Annual fishes / xerophils– ***Nothobranchias***.
12. Cave spawners is also called as ***Speleophils***.
13. Spawn in live invertebrates / ostrocophils – **Bitterlings** (*Rhodeus sericeus*)
14. Plant spawners – ***Polypterus***.
15. **Froth nesters** – Siamese fighter fish.
16. Hole-nesters – ***Cottusa leoticus***.
17. Miscellaneous material nesters are otherwise called as **Polyphils**.
18. Sand nesters – ***Cichlaso manicaraguense***.
19. Fore head brooders – ***Kurtius gullivers***.
20. Gill chamber brooder – ***Typhlichthys subterraneus***.
21. Pouch brooders – **pipe fish and sea horse**.
22. Mouth brooder – **tilapia**.
23. Arnold's lyre tail – ***Aphyosemion arnoldi***.
24. Neurohypophysis consists of nerve fibres, arising from the **perikaryon** of neurons, which are located in hypothalamus.

25. Seminal fluid through which the spermatozoa are released from the body is mostly secreted by cells lining the **epididymis and vas deferens**.
26. The technique of induction of breeding by administration of pituitary extract is called **hypophysation technique**.
27. Mauha oil cake contains **4-6% of saponin**.
28. Freshly hatched larva is called as **hatchlings or spawn**.
29. **Intramuscular injection** is done either on dorsal part of caudal peduncle or in the dorsal muscle above lateral line.
30. Kakabans – **egg collectors**.
31. **Carbamide solution** – removing the stickiness of egg.
32. **Sac fry** – eyed stage egg.
33. FSH – **gonadotropin**.
34. **Ovatide** – synthetic compound.
35. Prostaglandis – **follicle rupture**.
36. *Clarius gareipinus* – **African catfish**.
37. *C. macrocephalus* – **Asian catfish**.
38. *C. batrachus* – **Indian catfish**.
39. **Malachite green** – prophylactic measure.
40. Androgen – **male hormone**.
41. Brown trout – ***Salmo trutto fario***.
42. Rainbow trout – ***Onchorinchous mykiss***.
43. Golden mahseer – ***Tor puditora***.
44. Male golden fish – **Tubercles**.
45. **Common carp** contributed **7.98%** of total aquaculture production.
46. **Mechanical hatching** is the process in which egg envelops is broken down by mechanical action.
47. Hatchlings of ***Ictalurus punctatus*** are **golden** coloured and falls through the mesh of egg basket in to trough.
48. Males with oozing milt are called as **milter**.
49. Pituitary gland – **alcohol preservation**.
50. Physiological saline – **0.85% sodium chloride**.
51. **Synahorin** – synthetic hormone.
52. Ovatide – **20b- dihydroxy progesterone**.
53. Larval feed – **egg custard**.

54. Java tilapia – ***Oreochromis mossambicus***.
55. Duck mouth inlet – **hatching pool**.
56. Weedicide – **2, 4– dichlorophenoxy acetic acid**.
57. Saponin – **plant derivative poisons**.
58. Endrin- **chlorinated hydrocarbon**.
59. Malathion- **organophosphates**.
60. Beetles – **coleopteran**.
61. Notoenetids – **hemiptera**.
62. Dragon fly – **odonata**.
63. Silver carp – **bluish colour eggs**.
64. Grass carp – **golden brown colour eggs**.
65. One man method – **trout**.
66. California type trough – **trout hatchery**.
67. Mahseer – **coldwater fishes**.
68. Common gold fish – **metallic orange eggs**.
69. Barb – ***Barbus tetrazona***.
70. ***Epinephelus fuscoguttatus*** – brown marbled groupers.

5

Shellfish Hatchery Management

1. ***P. monodon*** (green tiger prawn) is the most candidate species for culture.
2. Testis have **6 lobe** all lobes are connected on the inner margin leading to vasdeferens.
3. Spermatozoa are stored in the **terminal of ampulae**.
4. Inhibitory hormone are secreted in the **early maturity** stage.
5. Matured ovary has dark color due to the accumulation of the **carotenoid pigment**.
6. The first abdomen segment assumed that have diamond shape called as **saddle**.
7. Male have petasma on the **first pair of pleopod**.
8. Female have thelycum on the **4 & 5th pair** of walking leg.
9. Male has Gonophore on the **fifth pair** of the walking leg.
10. Female has Gonophore on the **third pair** of walking leg.
11. The fecundity rate of range from **2-10 lakhs per female**.
12. The fertilized egg is called as **zygote**.
13. **Flow cytometer** is method used to monitor the **fertilization rate**.
14. A newly hatched larvae is **0.34mm** in size dark yellow in colour and have **3 pairs of appendages.**
15. The duration of nauplius stage is **36-48 h**.
16. Protozoa start the **feeding**.
17. After **20-22 molt** shape body and appendages resemble that of adult
18. The first successful breeding and larvae rearing was done by the **Hudinaga**.
19. Removal of eye stalk was firstly done by the **panouse** the interval between the eye stalk ablation and spawning is known as **latency period**.
20. *M. rosenbergii* commonly called as **scampi**.

21. **Raft** culture is under taken where water depth **above the 5 m depth**.
22. **Rack** culture is under taken where water depth is **below 5 m depth**.
23. The first captive breeding of fresh water prawn was done by the **S.W. Ling** but **perfected** by the **Fujimura**.
24. *M. rosenbergii* breeding in India was done by **Rajayalakshmi**.
25. South West monsoon influences – **Kerala coast**.
26. Growth in crustaceans – **depends on feed quality**.
27. Nursery ground for shrimp larvae – **Estuary**.
28. **MIH** – secreted by neurosecretary hormone.
29. Y-gland located in **antennary** and **maxillary** gland.
30. ***Scylla tranquebarica*** size of male- 133mm; female- 125mm.
31. Incubation period of crab – **15 days**.
32. Male lobster deposits spermatophores in **sternum** of female.
33. Newly hatched crab larvae – **1.2 mm**.
34. Length of 5^{th}zoea stage of crab is **3.5 mm**.
35. **Exuvia** – shed off shell.
36. Moulting is induced by **ecdysone**.
37. Moulting is **controlled** by **MIH**.
38. Shrimps breed in **deep sea**.
39. Eyestalk ablation done in shrimps for **induced maturation**.
40. **Crustacean maturation** depends on light; hormone; feeding and water quality.
41. Lobsters **carry** their eggs during **incubation**.
42. Seed production technique for **sand lobster** (*Panulirus americanus*) was standardized in **U.S.A**.
43. Y Gland responsible for regulating **moulting** in shrimp.
44. Fresh water seed production technology was first described by **S.W.Ling**.
45. **Gonopore** is an opening used for release of **gamete** in crustaceans.
46. **Inhaling or siphoning** is a process by which oysters takes in water.
47. Vertical transmission is a disease transmitted from **brood stock to larva**.
48. Testes of penaeids have **6 lobes**.
49. Lobster breeding cycle – **250 days**.

50. Gonad shape of lobster – **H shape**.
51. Shrimp larvae prefer ***Skeletonema* and *Tetraselmis***.
52. Oyster larval feed – ***Isochrysis galbana**, Pavlova dicartia and all phytoflagellates*.
53. Luminescence in hatchery is caused by ***Vibrio harveyi* and *V.alginolyticus***.
54. Common inducing agents in hatchery – **H_2O_2, NaOH,** NH_3OH and **Tris Buffer**.
55. Fresh water prawn **does not require** eyestalk ablation.
56. **Inter-moult** period is a right period of eyestalk ablation.
57. **Silver nitrate** is a chemical used in electro cauterization.
58. MIH/ GIH are **prevented** by eyestalk ablation.
59. Larval stage of edible oyster is **5**.
60. **Diatoms** and **microalgae** are basic feeds for pearl oyster larvae.
61. Fresh water prawn breeds in **brackish water**.
62. The post larva of oyster is called as **spat**.
63. Feeding nature of protozoea (*Penaeus monodon*) is **herbivores**.
64. **AG** – Androgenic hormone.
65. **AHT** – Artemia Hatching Tank.
66. Casting of old shell and forming new exoskeleton is called as **moulting**.
67. Sperm receiving organ in female is called as **seminal receptacle**.
68. Removal or extirpation of organ is called as **ablation**.
69. **Latency period** is the interval between eyestalk ablation and spawning.
70. Sex ratio for shrimps under captivity is **1:2** (Male: Female).
71. Prawn that lives only in fresh water – ***M.choprai***.
72. Prawn that lives only in sea water – ***Metapenaeus oceanica***.
73. The shrimp that doesn't come to estuarine phase – **Kiddi shrimp**.
74. Larval stage of prawn – **11**.
75. Larval stage of *P.monodon* - **12**.

6

Culture of Fish Food Organisms

1. Catla prefers **zooplankton**.
2. Silver carp prefers **phytoplankton**.
3. The blooming of diatoms causes **golden brown** colour in the aquaculture system.
4. Light or bright green colour of pond is due C***hlorella*** (Green algae).
5. **Dark green** or blackish green colour is due to BG algae (*Oscillatoria, Phormidium, Microcoleus*).
6. Dark brown colour or **sauce like** colour is due to **eutrophication**.
7. Yellowish colour of pond water is due to growth in ***Chrysophyta***.
8. **Foggy white** colour of pond is denoted by the mixture of zooplankton, clay particles and detrirus.
9. **Japan** is the biggest producer of marine **finfish fry** of 200 million fry per year (*Pagrus major, Paralichthys olivaceus* makes up 70% of total production).
10. **Europe** is a **second** biggest producer of marine fish fry for about 100 million fry per year.
11. **Phycology** is a scientific study of algae.
12. The Greek word ***phykos*** – *seaweed.*
13. **Chatoceros** is the largest genus of marine planktonic diatoms (approx. 400 sp).
14. **Chrysophyceae** – Golden yellow flagellate.
15. **Haptophyceae** – Golden brown flagellate.
16. **Cyanophyceae** – Blue green algae.
17. **Cladocera** – Water fleas.
18. ***Daphnia*** is used as a food source in the freshwater larviculture.
19. *Moina* was first described by **W.Baird** in 1850.
20. ***Brachionus calyciflorus*** and ***B.rubens*** are the most commonly cultured rotifers in fresh water mass culture.

21. ***B.pilicatilis*** and ***B.rotundiformis*** are the saline rotifers cultured across the world.
22. **TMRL medium** – stands for Tung Kang Marine Research lab.
23. Axenic culture – **sterile medium**.
24. Size of Micro plankton – **20 to 200 µm**.
25. Size of Nano plankton – **10 to 20 µm**.
26. Size of Ultra plankton – **2 to 10 µm**.
27. Size of Pico plankton – **less than 2 µm**.
28. The mesh size for collecting **infusoria** and **smaller rotifers** – 80 µm.
29. The mesh size for collecting larger rotifers, nauplius, epipodite stages of copepods – **160 µm**.
30. The mesh size for collecting smaller water fleas, **cyclopoid** copepods – 300 to 500 µm.
31. The mesh size for collecting **Daphnia** and larger **calanoid** copepods – 700 µm.
32. Order of rotifers – **Monogononta**.
33. Head of the rotifers carries **corona**.
34. **Lorica** is a kertain like proteins found in the epidermal layer of rotifers.
35. The small strain of rotifer – **130 to 340 µm**.
36. The larger strain of rotifer – **100 to 201 µm**.
37. Sexual reproduction of rotifers is called as **mictic** reproduction.
38. Under stress condition, female rotifer may produce about **20 amictic** eggs.
39. In 1967, **Hirata** and **Mori** introduced the use of **baker's yeast** in the rotifer culture.
40. Young nauplius of artemia is **positively phototactic**.
41. The artemia adults are **negatively phototactic**.
42. In artemia, vertical and horizontal distribution patterns are completely **different** during day and night time.
43. Brine shrimp grows from **larvae to adult** in less than 2 weeks.
44. **Cryptobiosis** – (hidden life) the cysts of artemia are metabolically inactive and can remain in total stasis for 2 years in dry oxygen free conditions, even at temperatures below freezing.
45. The nauplius of artemia is less than **0.4 mm** in length when they first hatch.

46. Cyst (0.2 to 0.3 mm) hatches in **low saline** waters (i.e. 5ppt).
47. Protein content of Spirulina – **60 to 70%.**
48. Red wiggler – ***Eisenia foetida***.
49. European night crawler – ***Eisenia hortensis***.
50. African night crawler – ***Eudrilus eugeniae***.
51. Brown algae contain **iodine** and **align**.
52. Red algae is a source of **agar**.
53. Fresh water infusoria **Paramecium.**
54. Marine water infusoria – **Fabrea & Euplotes.**
55. Rotifer commonly called as **Wheel animalcule**.
56. **Baker's yeast** is mostly used as the main diet ingredient for rotifer.
57. Artemia also known as **Brine shrimp**.
58. Cladocerans commonly called as **Water flea**.
59. Daphnia contain **70% more protein.**
60. Diatom – **Chaetoceros**.
61. Replacement for Artemia – **Moina**.
62. Spirulina has protein content about **62- 68 %.**
63. The gastropod groups of **Mollusca** can be called as **grazer.**
64. Chlamydomonas is a **unicellular** algae.
65. The **calcium** content in kelp are more than in milk.
66. Porphyra also known as **Nori** or **laver.**
67. Nori contain maximum protein content of **35-45 %**.
68. **Deterpenes** obtained from brown algae.
69. **Betains** obtained from green algae.
70. **Erythrotrichia** commonly known as **red bloom**.
71. In diatom **upper** valve known as **epitheca**, lower valve known as **hypotheca**.
72. **Dunaliella** algae have rich vitamin.
73. PBR- photo bioreactor mainly designed for maintain **mono algal culture**.
74. Spirulina protein contains phycocyanin, is marked as **Lina blue**.
75. Dunaliella first suggested as commercial source for **glycerol.**
76. CFTRI- central food technology research institute in **Mysore.**
77. In fresh water microcystis **Anabaena blooms** are cause mass **mortality**.

78. Microcystis produce **neurotoxin.**
79. Original definition for plankton was given by **Henson.**
80. In cladocerans **males are smaller** and have shorter life span.
81. Ostracods usually called as **seed shrimp**.
82. Copepod are **less than half of millimeter**.
83. Infusoria comes under the class **ciliates**.
84. ***B. plicatilis*** is euryhaline species.
85. Most predominant mode reproduction for rotifer **parthenogenesis**.
86. The chlorella mass culture is done by using **F medium.**
87. The Artemia was first reported by **Lymington** in England in 1755.
88. Artemia also called as brine worm, **sea monkey**.
89. Adult Artemia measuring about **1-2 cm** length.
90. Artemia have **13 larval stage**.
91. The **first stage larvae** is best for larval feed.
92. **CYCLOP-EEZE** has much higher concentrations of essential **omega - 3** fatty acid.
93. Moina has length about **0.5 - 1 mm**.
94. Daphnia have length about **0.5 - 2.5 mm**.
95. Daphnia & Moina reproduce **parthanogenitically**.
96. Cladocerons young one are released in small batches known as **clutches**
97. **Phased fertilization** was developed for cladocerans.
98. **Tubifex, chironomid** are commonly used as live food for the maintaining of ornamental fishes.
99. Tubifex - **sludge worm**
100. Chironomid – **blood worm**
101. Tubifex are commonly available in **sewage drain**
102. The Tubifex worm eggs are called as **cocoon**
103. Micro algae ranging from **5 - 25 micron** size
104. Common name for thalassiosira psedunana is **3H**
105. Life span of rotifer **5 - 7 days**
106. ***B. plicatilis*** eat chlorella, Tetraselmis
107. The special eggs of cladocerans known as **ephippia**
108. The best feed for daphnia are **Nano planktonic algae**
109. Fairy shrimp - **anostracans**

7

Fish Nutrition and Feed Technology

1. Feed costs **40 - 60%** of the operational cost of the aquaculture systems.
2. Nutrition consists of **diet** (what you take in) and **metabolism** (what happens to it after it enters your body).
3. Types of nutrients: **6** (water, protein, lipid, carbohydrate, vitamin and minerals).
4. **Organic nutrients** – Carbohydrates, Fats, Proteins and Vitamins.
5. **Inorganic nutrients** – Minerals.
6. Energy yielding nutrients – **Protein, Fat and Carbohydrates**.
7. Non-Energy yielding nutrients – **Vitamin and Mineral**.
8. Lower protein requirement – **Herbivores and omnivores**.
9. Higher protein requirement – **Carnivores**.
10. Average calorific values for protein – **5.65 Kcal/ g**.
11. Average calorific values for Carbohydrate – **4.15 Kcal/ g**.
12. Average calorific values for lipids – **9.45 Kcal/ g**.
13. **Energetics** is the study of energy requirements and flow of energy within the system.
14. **Gross energy** – energy released as heat when substance is completely oxidised to carbon di-oxide, Nitrous oxide or water.
15. Gross energy can be determined by **bomb calorimeter**.
16. **Digested energy** = Intake energy – Faecal energy.
17. Metabolizable energy = Intake energy – (Faecal energy + Urinary energy + Gill excretion energy).
18. Total heat production is the energy lost from the animal in the form of heat.
19. Heat increment is also called as **SDA**.
20. SDA is abbreviated as **Specific Dynamic Action**.
21. **SDA** is the increase in heat production followed by consumption of food by an animal in a **thermo-neutral environment**.

22. The aim of nutrition in aquaculture is to **maximize Retained energy** and **minimize all other energy losses** in a cost effective manner.
23. Essential amino acids are also called as **indispensable amino acids**.
24. Non-essential amino acids are also called as **dispensable amino acids**.
25. The required amino acids must be provided in the diet to achieve **optimum growth**.
26. Deficiency in essential amino acids leads to can **limit protein synthesis**.
27. **Tryptophan** deficient leads to scoliosis.
28. **Methionine** deficient leads to lens cataract.
29. Protein requirement of herbivorous and omnivorous fish is about **25 to 35 %**
30. Protein requirement of carnivorous fish is about **40 to 50 %**.
31. The **younger** animal generally requires **higher** levels **of protein** than older animals (5 - 10% of protein).
32. Asian catfish – ***Clarius batrachus***.
33. African catfish – ***Clarius garepinus***.
34. Snake head fish – ***Channa micropeltes***.
35. Yellow tail – ***Seriolaquin queradiata***.
36. Plaice – ***Pleuronectes platessa***.
37. Striped bass – ***Morone saxatilis***.
38. Estuary grouper – ***Epinephelus salmoides***.
39. Gilthead bream – ***Pagrus auratus***.
40. Red sea bream – ***Pagrus major***.
41. The dietary lipid for fishes – **8 to 10 %**.
42. The dietary lipid for carnivorous fishes – **15 to 20 %**.
43. **Triglycerides** – provides **concentrated source of energy** for aquatic species.
44. **Phospholipids** – responsible for the **structure of cell membranes** (i.e. Lipid bi-layer).
45. Shrimp require **phospholipid** for growth, moulting, metamorphosis and maturation.
46. Lipids of squid, clam, shrimp, fish and polychaetes are excellent natural source of **phospholipids**.
47. **Soylecithin** is also a source of phospholipids.

48. Crustaceans like shrimp require **dietary cholesterol** (0.5 to 1.25%) which is **not essential for fish**.
49. Marine invertebrate oils are rich source of **cholesterol**.
50. Saturated fatty acids – **not** have double bonds.
51. Unsaturated fatty acids – have one or more double bonds.
52. PUFA – **2 to 4 double** bonds.
53. HUFA – **5 to 6 double** bonds.
54. EFA – essential for cellular metabolism.
55. **Shock syndrome** – loss of consciousness for a few seconds followed by an acute stress.
56. Marine fish require **n - 3 HUFA** for optimal growth and health (0.5 – 2.0 %).
57. EPA = **20:5n - 3**
58. DHA = **22:6n - 3**
59. Linolenic acid = **18:3n - 3**
60. Linoleic acid = **18:2n - 6**
61. General formula for omega nomenclature is **X:Yn - Z**
62. **Monosaccharides** – Glucose and fructose.
63. **Disaccharides** – Sucrose and maltose.
64. Digestible polyseaccharides – **Starch and glycogen**.
65. Structural polysaccharides – Chitin, cellulose and others.
66. Oligosaccharides – **Raffinose** and **stachyose**.
67. The dietary carbohydrate level of **herbivorous** fish **25%**
68. The dietary carbohydrate level of **omnivorous** fish **45%**
69. The dietary carbohydrate level of **carnivorous** fish less than **20%**
70. The dietary carbohydrate level of shrimp **25 - 35%**
71. Thiamine (B1) – **Carbohydrate metabolism**.
72. Riboflavin (B2) and Niacin – **Hydrogen transfer**.
73. Pyridoxine (B6) - **Protein metabolism**.
74. Pantothenic acid – **Lipid** and **Carbohydrate** metabolism.
75. Biotin – **Carboxylation** and **decarboxylation**.
76. Choline – **Lipotrophic factor** and component of cell membranes.
77. Folic acid – **Single carbon metabolism**.

78. Cyanocobalamin (B12) – **Red blood cell formation**.
79. Vitamin C – **protein synthesize**.
80. Vitamin D – **Ca and P metabolism**.
81. **Ascorbic acid** – Blood clotting and collagen synthesis.
82. **Inositol** – Component of cell membranes.
83. Micro minerals are called as **trace minerals**.
84. The bulk of fish meal production comes from **anchovy fishery**.
85. **Fish silage** – **Formic acid** fermented mixture of fish waste.
86. The major synthetic amino acids available for supplementation are **L-lysine** and **DL-methionine**.
87. The commonly available commercial antioxidants are **BHT** (200 ppm), **BHA** (200 ppm) and **ethoxyquin** (150 ppm).
88. Preservatives – sodium or potassium salts of propionic, benzoic or sorbic acid.
89. Synbiotics – **probiotics + prebiotics**.
90. Grinders are used to reduce the size of the feed ingredients.
91. Mills are used to **mix** the feed ingredients.
92. **Hammer mill** is best suited for **aqua feed preparation**.
93. **Surge bins** are referred as temporary **storage bins**.
94. The density range of floating aquatic feeds – 320 to 400 g/ l.
95. The density range of sinking aquatic feeds – **400 to 600 g/ l**.
96. The density range of slow sinking aquatic feeds – **390 to 410 g/ l**.
97. In aquaculture practices, feed cost of carp farming is about **30 - 50 %**.
98. In aquaculture practices, feed cost of shrimp farming is about **50 - 80%**.
99. Annual growth of the aquaculture production is about **9%**.
100. The **feed supplies** the **dietary requirements** for the organisms.
101. Natural feed is also called as **live feed** or **viable feed**.
102. examples of live feed - **Unicellular and filamentous algae**.
103. Favorite food for milk fish – **Lab lab** (blue green algae).
104. Favorite food for mullet – **Lumut** (filamentous green algae).
105. Rotifers – **wheel animalcules**.
106. **Cladocerans** – Daphina spp. Moina spp.
107. **Copepods** – Calanus spp., Cyclops spp.

108. **Anostracans** are commonly known as **fairy shrimp.**
109. Mud eaters – **chironomids.**
110. Artificial feeds are classified as purified or semi-purified diets and practical diets.
111. CMC – **Carboxyl Methyl Cellulose.**
112. Fingerlings feeds – **Grower feed.**
113. Grow out feeds – **Finisher feed.**
114. Product quality – Specific purpose food.
115. Dry feed – **7-13 % moisture** content.
116. the two types of dry feedare **Floating and sinking** feeds.
117. Semi moist feed – **15 to 25%** of moisture content.
118. Moist feed – **26 to 45%** of moisture content.
119. Wet feed – **46 to 70%** of moisture content.
120. The feed which is supplement with the natural food source is called **supplementary feed.**
121. The feed which supply all major and minor nutrient to compensate their requirement is called as **complete feed.**
122. Lengthwise fold present in the intestine is called as **typhosole.**
123. Transverse fold present in the intestine is called as **rugae.**
124. Finger like projections in the intestine is called as **villi.**
125. Minnow fish lack **gastric gland.**
126. Fish gizzard does not have **digestive glands.**
127. Gastric glands **occur** in most of the **predatory** fishes.
128. Gastric glands secrete gastric juice which contains **HCl** and **Pepsinogen.**
129. pH of gut – **2.4 to 3.6.**
130. Liver – **largest gland** secretes bile juice.
131. **Gall bladder** act as a **storehouse** for continuously secreting **bile.**
132. Bile pigments – **Billierdin** and **bilirubin.**
133. **Liver** acts as a storage organ of **fats** and **vitamin A & D.**
134. Glandular organ – **Pancreas.**
135. Pancreas is formed of **Exocrine and Endocrine tissue.**
136. pH of pancreatic duct is from **neutral to alkaline.**
137. **Inactive** form of trypsin is called as **Trypsinogen.**

138. Small intestine secretes a group of aminopeptides and dipeptides (erepsin).
139. Intestinal fluid contains 3 inverting enzymes called as **Maltase, Lactase** and **Sucrase**.
140. The passage of food through the lining of the digestive tract into the blood is called as **absorption**.
141. **Carnivores** – Sea bass, Trout, Eel, Salmon, Freshwater shark, Catfish and Murrel.
142. **Herbivores** – Grass carp, Silver carp and Milk fish.
143. **Omnivores** – Common carp and Shrimp.
144. **Detritivores** – Mullet.
145. Grazers – **Parrot fishes** (Biting habitat).
146. Strainers – **Plankton eating fishes**.
147. Suckers – **presence of inferior mouth** and sucking lips.
148. 50% of Carbon + 16% of Nitrogen + 21.50% of Oxygen + 6.50% of Hydrogen = **protein**.
149. The empirical formula of amino acid is **R-CH-NH_2-COOH**.
150. The gross energy of the protein is **5.60 K Cal/ g**.
151. Collagen, elastin and keratin are **fibrous protein**.
152. **Globular protein** = Albumins, globulin and histones.
153. **Conjugated proteins** = Glycoprotein, lipoprotein, Metallo protein, phospho proteins, chromo proteins, nucleo proteins and cell nucleus.
154. Mono amino mono carboxylic acids – Glycine, Valine, Threonine, Leucine, Isoleucine.
155. Mono amino di carboxylic acids – **Aspartic acid, Glutamic acid**.
156. Di amino mono carboxylic acids – **Arginine, Lysine**.
157. Aromatic and heterocyclic amino acids – Phenyl alanine, Tyrosine, Tryptophan, Histidine and Proline.
158. Protein requirement for marine shrimp – **20-25%**.
159. Protein requirement for catfish – **28 to 32%**.
160. Protein requirement for tilapia – **32 to 38%**.
161. Protein requirement for hybrid striped bass – **38 to 42%**.
162. Carnivorous fish need **40 to 50 %** of proteins.
163. Omnivorous fish need **25 to 35%** of proteins.

164. Kjeldahl method, Biuret method, Folin-lowry method are the different types of **protein estimation**.
165. **Methionine** and **Phenylalanine** are amino acids which can be partially replaced or spared by two non-essential amino acids namely, **cysteine** and **tyrosine**.
166. **Methionine** and **lysine** are the first two limiting amino acids in the feed.
167. Methionine and cysteine – **sulphur amino acids**.
168. Mung, red beans **(legumes)** are high in **lysine**.
169. The calorific value of fat – **8 to 9.5 K Cal/ g**.
170. Glycerolipids – Glycolipids, Galactolipids.
171. Phospholipids – **Lecithins, Cephalins**.
172. **Sterols** are the main **precursors of sex** and other hormone
173. **Palmitic acid and oleic acids** are **monounsaturated** fatty acids
174. **Arachidonic and linoleic acids** are highly **unsaturated** fatty acid
175. **EPA, DHA** & linolenic acids are highly unsaturated fatty acid (omega 3)
176. "n - 3"- **linolenic acid**.
177. "n - 6"- **linoleic acid**.
178. **Marine fish** require n-3 HUFA for optimum growth about **0.5 - 2 % of dry diet**
179. Two major groups EFA is **EPA & DHA**.
180. **EFA deficiencies** are more **noticeable** in **seawater** than in freshwater condition
181. **Cold water species** appears to have a **greater requirement for "n-3" fatty acids** than warm water species
182. **Carbohydrate** are the most **economic inexpensive** source of energy
183. Fish can only extract **1.6 k cal from 1g** of carbohydrate
184. **Carnivorous** fishes are **not able** to efficiently convert the carbohydrate
185. **Channel catfish , shrimp** can **able** to convert the complex carbohydrate
186. The basic unit of carbohydrate are known as **monosaccharides**.
187. Glucose, fructose are **monosacharides**.
188. Sucrose, maltose, lactose are **disaccharides**.
189. Dextrin, starch are **poly saccharide**.
190. Chitine, cellulose, glycogen are **homopolysaccharide**.
191. Gums are **heteropoly** saccharides

192. **Fresh water** and **warm water** species are generally able to **utilize** higher level of dietary **carbohydrate**.
193. In fish glucose in blood returns to normal at least **7 hours**.
194. Carnivorous species diet should contain CHO level **less than 20%**.
195. Omnivorous & herbivorous species are capable of utilizing **40-45% of CHO**.
196. GNOC &RB contain as high as 45% of CHO
197. For **chitin synthesis** and **NEFA synthesis** the carbohydrate is more important
198. Precursor of chitin - **glucosamine**
199. Carbohydrate level in semi intensive culture system needs **25-30%**.
200. CHO level in extensive culture system needs **35-40%**.
201. Water soluble vitamins 11 numbers.

     B1-thiamine

     B2-riboflavine

     B6-pyridoxine

     B12- cynocobalamine
202. Vit C is the most important because it is **powerful antioxidant** & helps the immune system.
203. The most common vitamin deficiency in fish nutrition is that of **vit B**.
204. **Thiaminase** level **of fresh water** fish flesh are higher **than** in that of marine fish.
205. Vit B1 control the **CHO metabolism**.
206. Vit B6 involved in **transamination,** deamination, **decarboxylation**.
207. **Black Death problem** occurred due to **ascorbic acid deficiency**.
208. Vitamin D_2 – **Ergocalciferal**.
209. Vitamin D_3 – **Cholecalciferol**.
210. Sources of vitamin D is fish liver oils, liver meals and fish meal.
211. Vitamin K naturally occur in **two forms** namely K_1 in plants and K_2 in microorganisms.
212. Synthetic forms of **vitamin K (K_3 – Menadione)** is required for normal blood coagulation of the blood in animals.
213. Wet feed contain moisture content **about 50 - 70%**.
214. Most formulated feed with moisture content of **20 - 40 %**.
215. Precursor of vitamin A – **lypoxygenase**

Fisheries Resource Management

8

Taxonomy of Fishfish

1. **Taxon** – group of organisms in a classification and given biological names.
2. **Category** – the **level or rank** at which the taxon is placed.
3. **Systematics** is a biological science that discovers names, determines relationships, classifies and studies evolution of living organisms.
4. Alpha taxonomy – **description of new species**.
5. Beta taxonomy – relationships are worked outon the **species level** and on higher categories.
6. Gamma taxonomy – studying the **intraspecific variations** and its evolutionary relationship.
7. Right eye flounders – **Pleuronectidae & Soleidae**.
8. Left eye flounders – **Bothidae & Cyanoglossidae**.
9. Cyanoglossidae – **Tongue sole** (only pelvic fin present and **absence of pectoral fins**)
10. **Morphometric** characters are **measurable** characters
11. **Standard length** is a linear measurement taken from the tip of **the snout to the** tip of the **hypural bone**.
12. **Head length** is a linear measurement taken from the tip of the snout to the tip of the **posterior edge of the operculum**.
13. Meristic characters are **countable** characters
14. **Alizarin** staining of bones is used for the identification of bones
15. Order ends with – **formes**
16. Superfamily ends with – **oidea**
17. Family ends with – **dae**
18. Tribe ends with – **ini**
19. Any demonstrably intentional change in the original spelling of a name is **emendation**

20. The single specimen is identified as the type by the original author at the time of publication of the original description is called as **holotype**
21. Paratopotype is also called as **isotype**
22. ***Nomen nudum*** is a species name published **without satisfying the condition** of availability of the species
23. ***Nomen dubium*** is a species name having **insufficient recognition**.
24. ***Nomen oblitum*** is a name of species remained unused for more than fifty years.
25. ***Nomen conservandum*** is a name preserved by the action of commission and placed in an appropriate list
26. The purpose of the key is to facilitate identification of a **taxon**
27. keys are not phylogenies
28. **Centromeric index** $= \frac{\text{length of shorter arm of a chromosme}}{\text{total length of that chromosme}}$
29. **Arm ratio** $= \frac{\text{length of the long arm}}{\text{length of the short arm}}$
30. Relative length of a chromosme

$$= \frac{\text{length of a chromosme}}{\text{total length of all chromosme in the haploid set}} * 100$$

31. The term electrophoresis comes from the **Greek** and means "Transport by electricity"
32. **Eye lens protein** is employed as a valid character to **separate closely related species**.
33. **Congeneric** is a term refers to species of a **same genus**.
34. **Conspecific** is a term applied to individuals or populations of the **same species**
35. **Patronymic** is a dedicatory name based on the person to species in nomenclature
36. **Race** is a term which denotes a category below subspecies
37. **Spiracle** is an **opening behind the eye of the shark** and rays to let the water in
38. Heterodontidae – **Bullhead sharks**.
39. **Orectolobiformes** – **Carpet sharks**.
40. Rhincodontidae – **Whale sharks**.

41. Stegostomatidae – **Zebra sharks**.
42. Hemiscyllidae – **Bamboo sharks**.
43. Ginglymostomatidae – **Nurse sharks**.
44. Carcharhiniformes – **Ground sharks**.
45. Carcharhinidae – Requeim sharks.
46. Lamniformes – **Mackerel sharks**.
47. Alopidae – **Thresher sharks**.
48. Cetorhinidae – **Basking sharks**.
49. Chlamydoselachidae – **Frill sharks**.
50. Hexanchidae – **Cow sharks**.
51. Squalidae – **Dogfish sharks**.
52. Echinorhinidae – **Bramble sharks**.
53. Squantiniformes – **Angel sharks**.
54. Pristiophoridae – **Saw sharks**.
55. Rajiformes belongs to Skates and rays.
56. Rhinobatidae – **Guitarfishes**.
57. Rajidae – Skates.
58. Dasyotidae – **Stingrays**.
59. Urolophidae – **Round sting rays**.
60. Gymnuridae – **Butterfly sharks**.
61. Myliobatidae – **Eagle rays**.
62. **Mobulinae** is a subfamily containing manta and devil rays.
63. Class 1: Acanthodii – Spinous form – **Fossil fishes**.
64. Class 2: Sarcopterygii – **Lobe finned fishes** – Fossil fishes.
65. Class 3: Actinopterygii – **Ray finned fishes** – All commercially important fishes.
66. Sarcopterygii and Actinopterygii are together called as Euteleostomi or **Osteichthyes**.
67. ***Latimera chaluminae*** (living fossil) is found in western waters and limited to **African water bodies**.
68. Acipenseridae – **Sturgeon fish**.
69. Polyodontidae – **Paddlefish**.
70. Lepisosteidae – **Gar fish**.

71. Amiidae – **Bow fin**.
72. Osteoglossidae – **Bony tongues**.
73. Notopteridae – **Knife fishes**.
74. Mormyroidae – **Elephant fish**.
75. Elopidae – **Tenpounders / Lady fish**.
76. Megalopidae – **Tarpons**.
77. Acanthuridae – **Surgeon fish**/ Unicorn fish (1/ 2 bony plates on the either side of the caudal peduncle).
78. Anguillidae - **Fresh water eels**.
79. Ariidae – **Marine cat fish**.
80. Belonidae – **Needle fish**.
81. Chaetodontidae – **Butterfly fish**.
82. Chanidae – **Milk fish**.
83. Chirocentridae – **Wolf herrings**.
84. Citharidae – **Flounders**.
85. Clupeidae – Herrings, Shads, Sardines and Sprats (**no lateral** line present and presence of scutes along belly).
86. Coryphaenidae – **Dolphin fishes**.
87. Diodontidae – **Porcupine fishes** (lateral line **inconspicuous & no pelvic fins**).
88. Drepanidae – Sickle fish (pectoral fins long and falcate).
89. Echeneidae - Remora/ Shark suckers/ **Disc fishes**.
90. Engraulidae – Anchovy (**Snout pig like projecting**, lower jaw under slung, no lateral line).
91. Ephippidae – **Spade fish** (Anal fin with **3 spines**).
92. Exocoetidae – Flying fish.
93. Gemalpylidae – Snake mackerels, Barracudas (detached fin lets behind dorsal and anal fins). (lateral line extended upto caudal fin base).
94. Gerreidae – **Silver biddies**, Mojarras.
95. Haemulidae – Grunts, Sweet lips, Rubber lips, Hot lips (scales present on entire head except in snout, chin and presence of chin pores).
96. Harpadontidae – **Bombay duck**.
97. *Harpadon nehereus* has **extended lateral line** beyond caudal fin lobe.
98. Hemiramphidae – **Halfbeaks** (lateral line running down from pectral fin)

99. Holocentridae – Squirrel fish, **Soldier fish**.
100. Istiophoridae – Bill fish, Spear fish, Marlins, Sail fish (no rakers on the gill arches, which **have 2 dorsal and 2 anal fins**)
101. Labridae – Wrasses, Hog fish, **Razor fish**
102. Lactariidae – **False trevallies**, Milk trevallies
103. Leiognathidae – Pony fish, Slip mouths, Tooth ponies
104. *Leiognathus bindus:* mouth pointing **forward or downward** when protracted and absence of canniform teeth
105. *Secutor ruconius:* mouth pointing **upward** when protracted
106. *Gazza achlamys:* mouth pointing **forward** and presence of **canniform** teeth
107. Lethrinidae – Emperors, pig face breams **(maxilla overlapping premaxilla)**
108. Lutjanidae – Snappers, Job fish (serrated preopercle, scales on cheek, preopercle, gill cover)
109. **Gular plate** located between arms of lower jaw in the family called **Megalopidae**
110. Monocanthidae – **Filefish**, leatherjackets
111. Monodactylidae – Moonies
112. Mugilidae – Mullets **(no lateral line)**
113. Mullidae – Goat fish (presence of **two** long un-branched **barbells** on chin)
114. **Muraenesocidae** – Pike congers.
115. Muraeniiidae – Morays.
116. Nemipteridae – Thread fin bream/ Monocle breams/ Dwarf monocle breams.
117. Ostracidae – Box fish/ Cow fish (*Lactoria cornuta*).
118. Platacidae – **bat fish**.
119. Plotosidae – **Stinging catfish**/ Coral catfish/ Eel catfish/ Barbel catfish.
120. Polynemidae – Thread fins/ Tassel fish
121. Pomocanthidae – **Angelfish**.
122. Pomocentridae – **Damselfish**.
123. Psettodidae – **Spiny turbots**.
124. Rachycentridae – **Cobias** (presence of 7 to 9 short and strong isolated spine).
125. Scaridae – **Parrot fish**.

126. Scatophagidae – **Scats**.
127. Sciaenidae – **Croakers**, Drums, Meagres
128. Scombridae – Albacores, Bonitos, Mackerels, seer fishes, Tunas and Wahoos (Fusiform body and finlets)
129. Serranidae – **Groupers** (Superior mouth)
130. Siganidae – Spine foots, **Rabbit fish**
131. Sillaginidae – presence of **1 opercular** spine and anal fin with 2 weak spine
132. Sparidae – pogies, **sea breams**, stumpnoses
133. Sphyraenidae – **Barracudas**
134. Stromatidae – Butterfish, silver pomfrets **(no pelvic fins)**
135. Synodontidae – **lizard fish**.
136. Syngnathidae – **Sea horses** and **Pipe fishes**.
137. Tetradontidae – **Puffer fish,** blow fish
138. Triacanthidae – **Tripod fish**.
139. Trichiuridae – Cutlass fish, Hairtails, Frost fish, scabbard fish.
140. Zanclidae – **Moorish idol.**
141. In *Stolephorus* scutes present in only in front of **pelvic fin** not in belly
142. Snout pig like projection in **anchovy**
143. In dolphin fish lateral line curved **upward** above the pectoral fin
144. Nematolosa have last **dorsal fin ray**.
145. Preopercula spine present in the **Pomacanthidae**.
146. In mugiliforms adipose **eye lids** present
147. In cyprinformes scales **absent in head region**.
148. Lizard fish have **adipose fin**.
149. Short spiny eel – ***Macrognathus*** sp
150. Zig zag eel- ***Macrognathus armatus***
151. Sea mouth – **Pagasidae**
152. Cornet fish – **Fistularidae**
153. False pipe fish /ghost spine – **Solenostomidae**.
154. In Italy fresh anchovy known as – **alici**
155. **John Ray** was the first person to use the word of specie and genus
156. Oil fish – ***Ruvettus*** sp.

9

Taxonomy of Shellfish

1. The name taxonomy was first proposed by **Candolle in 1813**.
2. The shellfish includes two highly diversified (i.e. phylum **Arthropoda** and phylum **Mollusca**).
3. The commercial formalin used for preservation of shellfishes is about 40% concentration and diluted to 8-10%.
4. Ostracoda is also called as **Seed or Mussel shrimps**.
5. Cladocereans is also called as **water flea**.
6. Argulus is commonly called as **carp lice**.
7. Balanus species belongs to sub-class **Cirripedia**.
8. Pill bugs and wood lice are comes under the order of **Isopoda**.
9. Gammarus is commonly known as **sand hoppers** belong to order **Amphipoda**.
10. Squilla is called as **Mantis shrimp** belongs to order **Stomatopoda**.
11. The term **Prawn** is used for the animals that live in Freshwater (this animal completes its life cycle only within the limit of fresh water).
12. The term **shrimp** is used for the animals that live in Marine-water (this animal completes its life cycle only within the limit of Marine-water).
13. Penaeidae, Pandalidae, Hippolytidae, Sergestidae and Palaemonidae are the families of commercially important shrimps and prawns.
14. **Sergestid** shrimps are scientifically called as ***Acetus indicus***.
15. Examples for true crabs: **Portunus**, Carcinus, **Uca**.
16. Examples for Spider crabs: **Macrocheira**, **Libinia**.
17. The name Mollusca (in the latin mollis = soft), was first used by French Zoologist, **Cuvier** in 1798.
18. The only living species in the class **Monoplacophora** is ***Neoplina galathea*** *and* ***Neoplinae wingi***.
19. The most of the species belonging to the class **Amphineura's** were found to be primitive **Molluscs**.

20. Chiton is usually called as **Sea mice** / coat of mail shell.
21. Prosobranchia is otherwise called as **Streptoneura**.
22. Archaegastropoda is otherwise called as **Aspidobranchia**.
23. Patella is otherwise called as **Limpet**.
24. *Haliotis* is otherwise called as **Ear shell** or Abalone.
25. Trochus is otherwise called as **Top shells**.
26. Mesogastropoda is otherwise called as **Pectinibranchia**.
27. *Lambislambis* is otherwise called as **five fingered chank/ common spider conch**.
28. Cypraea is otherwise called as **Jewels of sea**/ cowries.
29. Neogastropoda is otherwise called as **Stenopoda**.
30. *Aplsia* is also called as **Sea hare**.
31. Thecostomata is also called as Shelled **pteropods**.
32. Gymnostomata is otherwise called as **Nakedpteropods**.
33. ***Doris sp.*** Belongs to order **Nudibranchia**/ Acoela / True sea slugs.
34. Bivalvia also referred as **Pelecypoda**.
35. Sub phylum mandibulata consist of **6 classes**.
36. Ring of exoskeleton covered the segment of The crustaceans upper ring is known as **tergite**, ventral region known as **sternite**
37. Parthaoenesis frquently occurred in the **branchiopoda, ostracoda**
38. Cephalocaridea have **horse shoe** shaped head and **19 pairs appendages**.
39. **Eye** and **carapace** are absent in the cephalocrida
40. Example for the cephalocarida – sandersilla
41. The example for branchiopoda **artemia** and **daphnia**.
42. Artemia comes under the order – anastroa
43. Daphnia comes under the order – cladocera
44. Example for ostracoda – **cypris**
45. Fish lice – **branchura**
46. Goose neck barnacles – **lepas**
47. Eumalacostraca have **20 body segment**
48. Fresh water prawn comes under the **palomonidae**
49. In male lobster the first and second pair of pleopod are transformed into copulatory organ it is called as **copulatory stytes**
50. Hermid crab – ***Eupagurus***

51. Flower crab – ***p. peagicus***.
52. Herbst – ***Calappa lophos***.
53. Lambis, cypria comes under the **Mesogastropoda**.
54. *Turbinella pyrum* comes under the family – **Vasidae**.
55. Fan shell - ***Pinna bicolor***.
56. Squid comes under the family – **Teuthoidea**.
57. Nereic squid comes under the sub order **Myopsidae**.
58. Octopus contain **8 arms**.
59. Torson occur in **7 ways**.
60. The list of important scientific names and common names:

Shrimps		
	Scientific Name	**Common Name**
1.	*Fenneropenaeus meruiensis*	Banana shrimps
2.	*Fenneropenaeus penicillatus*	Red tail shrimps
3.	*Penaeus semisulcatus*	Green tiger shrimps
4.	*Metpenaeus affinis*	Jinga shrimps
5.	*Metapenaeus brevicornis*	Yellow shrimps
6.	*Metapenaeus mooceros*	Speckled shrimps
7.	*Parapenaeopsis stylifera*	Kiddi shrimps
Freshwater Prawns		
1.	*Macrobrachium rosenbergii*	Giant river prawn
2.	*Macrobrachium malcolmsonii*	Cauvery prawn
Lobsters		
1.	*Panulirus homarus*	Scalloped spiny lobsters
2.	*Panulirus ornatus*	Ornate spiny lobsters
3.	*Panulirus polphagus*	Mud spray lobsters
4.	*Panulirus penicillatus*	Pronghorn spiny lobsters
5.	*Panulirus versicolor*	Painted spiny lobsters
6.	*Puerulus sewelli*	Whip lobsters
7.	*Thenus orientalis*	Slipper
CRABS		
1.	*Scylla serrata*	Giant mud crab
2.	*Scylla tranquebarica*	Purple mud crab
3.	*Portunus pelagicus*	Flower crab / blue swimming crab
4.	*Portunus sanguinolentus*	Three spotted crab
5.	*Charybdis ferriata*	Cross crab
6.	*Calappa lophos*	Herbst

Bivalvia		
1..	*Perna viridis*	Green mussel
2.	*Perna indica*	Brown mussel
3.	*Pecten sp.*	Scallops
4.	*Crassostrea madrasensis*	Edible oysters
5.	*Pinctada fucata*	Pearl oysters
6.	*Placuna placenta*	Window pane oyster
7.	*Tridacna maxima*	Giant clam
8.	*Donax cuneatus*	Wedge shells
9.	*Meretrix meretrix*	Bay/Great clam
10.	*Katelysia opima*	Inflated clam
11.	*Dentalium sp.*	Elephant's tusk shell
Cephalopoda		
1.	*Sepia pharaonis*	Cuttlefish
2.	*Loligo duvaucelli*	Squid
3.	*Octopus aegina*	Octopus

10

Anatomy of Fish

1. Anatomy the word derived from **Latin word**.
2. Study of internal structure and organization of organisms known as **anatomy**.
3. The macroscopic study of organisms is known as **gross anatomy**.
4. The study of parental developmental anatomy is known as **developmental anatomy**.
5. The study of tissue is known as **histology**.
6. The study of organization of cell and sub cellular components known as **cell biology**.
7. The study of nervous system is known as **Neuro anatomy**.
8. Bottom feeder has sub **terminal** or **inferior** mouth.
9. Sturgeon **bottom feeder**.
10. Grouper and lion fish has **superior mouth**.
11. In half beaks the **lower jaw projects**.
12. Upper jaw elongated in **paddle fish**.
13. In needle fish both **jaw are elongated**.
14. **Dentaries** are the main toothed bone.
15. Teeth present in tongue ex **glossohyal & baasibranchials**.
16. In carnivore fishes gill rakers are **long and teeth like**.
17. The omnivore has **short and stumpy** gill rakers.
18. *Hilsa ilisha* is a **planktivore**.
19. Taste buds are rare in **carnivores**.
20. The herbivore and omnivore possess **short esophagus**.
21. The carnivore have **longest esophagus**.
22. **Liver** is the largest **digestive gland** in fish.
23. Lamprey, pipe fish, hagfish, **parrot fish don't have stomach**.
24. Mullet & gizzard shad have **3 layers of stomach**.

25. Stomach shapes in fishes **I,J,U,Y,V**.
26. The carnivore have **shortest intestine**.
27. The herbivore has highly **coiled intestine**.
28. Shark, **sturgeon**, lungfish and **latimera** have a **spiral valve** inside the intestine.
29. **Rectal gland** present in shark.
30. **Cloaca** is the **urogenital pore** present in sharks, ray and skates
31. Liver covers **20 – 30** % body weight
32. The foregut & hindgut are lined internally by **cuticle** called **intima**.
33. The mid gut is lined by **endoderm**.
34. True lips are absent in **gastropod**.
35. Radula located in the top of the **odontopore**.
36. A wide curved sac opens into the alimentary canal in **cephalopods** known as **caecum**.
37. Ink gland present **cephalopod**.
38. Fishes has **single circulation**.
39. Lung fish has **double circulation** system.
40. **Arteries** are carry blood **away** from the heart.
41. In blood, **plasma** contributes **55%**.
42. In haemoglobin haem content about **5 %**.
43. Freezing point blood for fresh water fishes **-0.6** degcelcius in marine **fishes - 0.75**.
44. Leptocephalus has **colorless blood**.
45. **Channichthyids** have **low** amount of haemoglobin.
46. Haemoglobin concentration in fish blood is **7-10g/ 100ml**.
47. **RBC** size larger in **elasmobranch**.
48. The heart of fishes known as **branchial heart**.
49. Heart of fish is **S** shape.
50. Conus arteries are present in **elasmobranches**, acipencer, polypterus, lung fish.
51. **Both** Conus and bulbus arteries are present in **Amia**.
52. In bony fish **only one branchial arteries** are present in the each gill arch.
53. In cartilage have **two efferent branchial artery.**

54. The circulatory system of crustacean is **lacunar** type.
55. Fresh water mussel – ***Unio*** sp.
56. Bivalve has **3 chambered heart**.
57. Larvae of polypterus have **external gills**.
58. Dipnoi have **4 pairs of external gills**.
59. A complete gill known as **holobranch**.
60. Actual seat gas exchange is **secondary gill lamella**.
61. **Tuna** have very **thin lamellar** walls.
62. The elasmobranches have lamellar thickness about **5-11 micron**.
63. In bony **fishes gill septa** are progressively reduced.
64. **Pseudobranchs** cannot function in respiratory **gas exchange**.
65. The process of violent sweeping of water over the gill lamellae.
66. In counter current flow, the blood flow is **opposite** to the water current.
67. In fast swimming fishes mouth & gill operculum remain open to breath is known as **ram ventilation**.
68. Lamprey has **7 pairs of gill pouches**.
69. In **larvae of lamprey** respiratory tube connected with **mouth & esophagus.**
70. The hag fish normally has **5-15 pairs of gill arch**.
71. In **elasmobranch** the blood and water flow in the **same direction**.
72. Podobranch or **foot gill** are present in **freshwater prawn**.
73. Each maxillipede bears **one podobranch and two arthrobranch**.
74. Arthrobranch also known as **joint gill**.
75. All the gills of freshwater prawn are **phyllobranchs**.
76. **Ctenidium** possesses both **aquatic as well as aerial** respiration.
77. In **loaches** and some cat fishes the part **alimentary canal** used for respiration.
78. **Rectum of the** American cat fish (collichthys) absorbs oxygen drawn in through the anus & hind gut.
79. **Buccopharyngeal cavity** serves as a respiratory surface (ex) **mudskipper**.
80. The **islets** are derived from the **secondary lamella of a gill filament**.
81. **Saccular** organ is found associated with their branchial chamber in (*Heteropneustes fossilis*).

82. The brain covered by extensive network of blood vessels called **choroid plexi**.
83. The hind brain is known as **rhomb encephalon**.
84. The olfactory bulb and olfactory lobe are present in ***Puntius ticto***.
85. Olfactory bulb only present in the -***Tor tor, Mystus seenghala***.
86. Shark has well developed ganglia – known as **geniculate lobes**.
87. The largest and most important part of the diencephalon is **hypothalamus**.
88. Ventral part of hypothalamus projects a pouch like growth known as **infundibulum**.
89. The top of infundibulum contain **pituitary gland** .
90. Optic tectum has **6 layer**.
91. In **elasmobranches** the size of **cerebellum is larger** than the cyclostomes.
92. Unpaired kidney found in **coelacanth**.
93. **Head kidney** is non excretory and **endocrine function**.
94. In crustacean **green gland** involved in excretion.
95. Largest part of the green gland **bladder**.
96. In Mollusca excretion is done by **renal organ** or nephridia.
97. **Keber's found** in bivalve involved in excretory function.
98. In cephalopod **heart is three chambered**.
99. Lamprey and hag fish have **protocercal tail**.
100. Leptocercal tail present in **lungfish**.
101. Cod have **isocercal tail**.
102. Sunfish have **geophycercal tail**.
103. In gobies testis is **small and thread** like.
104. In **notopterus** testis un paired
105. Vas deference is absent in **salmon & trout**.
106. Immature fish has **green colour ovary**.
107. Ripe fishes have **golden yellow colour ovary**.
108. In egg layer oviductal tissue is modified into shell gland (nidamental gland).
109. Notopteridae has **semi cytovarian** type ovary.
110. Nidamental sac present in **cephalopod**.
111. Open thelycum present **Litopenaus, aristeidae**.

112. Closed thelycum present in **penaeidae**.
113. **Amia, perca, wrasses** has **yellow** pigment in eye.
114. Rhodopsin, porphyropsin present in **retina**.
115. The larvae of lung fish having **fahrenholz** resembling the lateral line organ.
116. In shark and relatives **Otolith are small**.
117. Ampulla of lorenzini is present in the **head region of the sharks and rays**.
118. The receptors of lateral line system are known as **neuromast**.
119. Crustacean have compound eye, each small unit called **ommatidium**.
120. Ospheridum is a **chemoreceptor**.
121. Opening of crustacean heart known as **Ostia**.
122. In sciaenids, **otolith** and **swimblader** are large in size.

11

Biology of Fish

1. Giant tube worms – ***Riftia*** sp.
2. Novel mussels – ***Bathymodiolus*** sp.
3. The stock inside the marine protected areas is called **as Bank account**.
4. Cartilaginous fishes don't have **swim bladder**.
5. Non- endemic species – **Grass carp**.
6. Banned species – Tilapia.
7. Non- parasite fish – **Echinoderms**.
8. Non- Penaeid fishery – **Maharashtra**.
9. Maximum shellfish and finfish exploiting state in India is **Kerala**.
10. Small reservoir more in **Tamil Nadu**.
11. Small lake in Tamil Nadu is **ALLIYAR**.
12. Fish and shrimp were not able to synthesis **vitamin C**.
13. Cyprinids – **false stomach**.
14. Sea crab – ***Charybdis cruciata***.
15. Scale eating fish – **common carp**
16. Rohu – **Red colour** egg.
17. Mrigal – **Yellow Brownish** colour egg.
18. Silver carp – **bluish colour** egg.
19. Dactylogyrus – **Gill flukes**.
20. Dropsy is caused by **bacteria**.
21. Largest fresh water lake in India is **Kolleru**.
22. Largest saline water lake in India **is Sambhar**.
23. Common cap and mrigal **omnivores**.
24. Catla are **plankton feeder**.
25. Fresh water prawn are **omnivores**.
26. Butterfly fish fed on **coral**.

27. Tuna and deep sea fishes are **active predator**.
28. **Grouper, stone** fish are lie and weight predator.
29. Blue gill - ***lepomis*** sp.
30. **Herbivore** have long alimentary canal and coiled intestine.
31. **Carnivore** have straight intestine.
32. **Herring** moves up or down **100-200 m** during the diurnal cycle.
33. **Sword fish** moves from the surface to **600 m** between night and day.
34. **Contrantant** – migration against the water current.
35. **Denatant** migration with the water current.
36. Salmon - **anadromous**.
37. Eel – **catadromous**.
38. The fishes form a dence layer at 500-600 ftdowm during the day. "It is known as **deep sea scattering layer**".
39. Prawn eats the **tricodesmium** algae.
40. Indirect method for age determination is **length frequency method, hard parts**.
41. **Peterson method** is used to **check or confirm** other method of age determination.
42. Coral trout – ***plectopomus leopardus***.
43. Fully developed gonad are almost completely occupies the abdomen cavity. Leads lower the feeding rate it's known as **spawning fast**.
44. **Ganoid** scales are present in **sturgeons, gars, bowfin, paddle fish, bichirs**.
45. Samples of 6 scales are generally needed for the age determination.
46. If the sample scales **are thin** it should treated with **caustic soda**.
47. The scales are usually stained with **borax carmine, alizarine, alizarinesulphat**.
48. **Back calculation** technique used to measure the **fish growth**.
49. Otoliths are lodged in **pro-otic** bone. It found sacculus of inner ear.
50. There are 3 types of otoliths are present. They are **sagittal, lapillus, astriscus**.
51. One opaque zone and one hyaline zone are taken as **1 year zone**.
52. **Otolith** method is more **reliable** then the scale method.
53. **Gorged stomach** - organism of **inside can** be seen.

54. Commonly used fixatives are **2 - 5 % formalin**.
55. Fecundity length relationship **F = aL^b**.
56. Fecundity weight relationship **F = aw + b**.
57. Length – weight relationship **W = aL^b**.
58. The B value should **be 3**.
59. The K_n value should be **1**.
60. ***Clupea herrangus*** has stage of maturity **4 years**.
61. Lake trout spawn at **5-7 years**.
62. Seabass comes under the **centropomidae**.
63. Seabass are **Protoandrous**.
64. Sparidae & labridae are **protogynus** (grouper).
65. Amazon molly (*Poecilia formosa*).
66. Ovoviviparous – **don't have parental care**.
67. **Ostrocophils**- spwan in live invertebrate.
68. Cavespawner - **speleophils**.
69. Large quantity of yolk present in the **lithophils**.
70. Brazilian cat fish male has enlarged **lip as pouch**.
71. In tilapia **male are bigger** than the female.
72. In carps **females are bigger** than the male.
73. In sword fish last fin rays of anal fin modified into **gonopodium**.
74. Jenynsidae- anal **fin act as a penis**.
75. In shark **pelvic fin** are modified in to **clasper**.
76. In ***Clarius*** sp & ***Heteropneustes*** sp elongated and **developed cylindrical papilla**.
77. The female has **butten shaped** papilla.
78. Ovipositer present in **bittrlings**.
79. Synchronous hermaphroditism (eg) **pulmonate land snails, land slug**.
80. Oviparous sharks are **zebra shark, cat shark**.
81. Ovoviviparous sharks are **nurse, tiger, saw, great white**.
82. **"big bang"** spawners die after spawning.
83. Oogenesis under goes by **mitotic division**.
84. Star fish eggs are **holoblastic** (lamprey).
85. Meroblastic- teleost, dipnoi.

86. Larvae of polychaete **trochophore & nectochaeta**.
87. Parr is a fry of **salmon**.
88. Whale & dolphin eggs are **alecithal**. no yolk will be present
89. Stolephorus have **oval shape eeg**.
90. Segmented egg present in **clupidae & carangidae**.
91. Wide perivitelline space present in **sardinella**, ciprinidae
92. Filamented egg membrane present in **hemiramphus**.
93. Spiny egg membrane – **lizard fish**.
94. Ventral fin absent in eel.
95. Marine catfish are **mouth brooder**.
96. Common carp eggs **adhesive** in nature.
97. Marmaid's purse also known as **devil purse**.
98. Rays are **oviparous**.
99. Cuttle fish eggs having **heavy amount yolk**.
100. Chlorella has size about **2 - 10 micro meter**.
101. Daphnia known as "water flea". Usually **1 - 5 mm long**.
102. Artemia commonly called **sea monkey**.
103. The adult Artemia have **3 eyes**.
104. Sagita- **arrow worm**.
105. Lucifer are commonly called as **"ghost shrimp"**.
106. The scientific study of fish is called as **Ichthyology**.
107. Fish is composed of **10 different systems** of body organs that work in unison to make up the whole individual.
108. Forked tail is present in the fishes like **cyprinids and clupeids**.
109. Lunate tail is present in **pomprates** (stromatidae).
110. Truncated tail is present in **trout**.
111. Rounded tail is present in **Channiformes&Perciformes**.
112. Pointed tail is present in Amphipneus, **Coilia, Glossogobius**.
113. Tri-lobed tail is present in **Bombay duck**.
114. Epicercal tail is present in **Scoliodon**.
115. **Hypocercal tail** is present in **Exocetus**.
116. **Leptocercal** tail is present in **rays and skates**.
117. Protocercal tail is present in **Hag-fish**.

118. Diphycercal tail is present in **coelacanth and lung fish**.
119. **Obtuse snout** is present in **cyprinoidae**.
120. Fleshy protruded snout is observed in **eels**.
121. **Beak like snout** is observed in *Beloncancila* and *hemirampus.*
122. **Gastro-somatic index** is more in herbivorous fishes.
123. The gastric acidity in fishes is measured to be ranging from **2.4 to 3.6**.
124. **Charles Elton** has experimented in the productivity of the Webber lake of Wisconsin in U.S.A.
125. In ***Opheocephalus**,* the pharyngeal cavity is modified to folded respiratory organ called **pharyngeal diverticula**.

12

Physiology of Finfish and Shellfish

1. The word physiology was first used by **Greeks** around 600BC to describe a philosophical enquiry into natural things.
2. The word "physis" meaning **nature**.
3. The discovery of blood circulation by **William Harvey** in 1628.
4. **C.Bernad** (1813 - 78) who is considered as one of the **founder of physiology**.
5. The process of transport of an oxygen from outside air into the cells within tissues are called as **Respiration**.
6. **STPD** is abbreviated as standard pressure dry.
7. The gill arch along with the filaments is called as **gill**.
8. Haemoglobin is abbreviated as **Hb** or **Hgb**.
9. **Cephalopods** use haemocyanin- a copper containing protein for oxygen transportation.
10. **Protobranch** - the gill structure tends to occur in **primitive groups** and appears as a small leaf like structure.
11. **Filibranch** - thegill structure consists of individual filaments forming **w shaped structures**.
12. **Eulamellibranch** - W shaped gills with cross partitions **joining the filaments** to create water filled cavities in between them.
13. **Septibranch** - gills are only found in **poromyacea** a super family of **rock borers**.
14. Fish blood consist **2 - 3%** of body weight.
15. Mature red blood cells are **7μ** in diameter.
16. Fishes possess **2 kinds of Hb**.
17. **Monomeric Hb** units found in Agnatha and **Hag fishes**.
18. **Tetrameric Hb** units found in **higher** fishes.
19. A fish electrocardiogram (ECG) is a graphical representation of the electrical activity of the heart.
20. The different types of kidney of marine teleosts

S.No	Kidneys	Examples
1.	Type I	clupeidae
2.	Type II	Marine catfishes and eel
3.	Type III	Mugilidae, Belonidae, Scombridae, Carangidae, Pleuronectidae.
4.	Type IV	Sea horse and pipefish
5.	Type V	Lophius sp.

21. The **kidney of freshwater** fishes often **larger** in relation to body weight than that of marine fishes.
22. The excretory glands of the Crustacean is **antennal glands or maxillary glands.**
23. Crustaceans excrete through **nephridia**.
24. **Osmoregulation** is a physiological activity for proper maintenance of **water and salt** balance.
25. **Sparidae** and **Serranidae** are true hermaphrodites
26. **Parthenogenesis** is a process observed in **guppy &** (*Poeciliaformosa).*
27. The ovary wall is made up of **3 layers namely**, they are Outer Peritonium, Middle Albuginea, and Inner Epithelium.
28. Baby sharks called **pups**.
29. Living muscle is composed of many long cylindrical staped fibres from **0.02 to 0.08 mm** in diameter.
30. Lateral line canals contain sensory cells called **pit organs**.
31. Blind cave fish – ***Astyanax mexicanus***.
32. Pineal gland is also called as **light-sensitive organ (third eye)**.
33. The light-sensitive pigment called **rhodopsin**.
34. Metabolism = **Catabolism+Anabolism**.
35. The hormones of urophysis are called as **urotensins**.
36. **Adrenal gland is not** present in most of the fishes.
37. Surgical removal of the pituitary gland is called as **hypophysectomy**.
38. Chromaffin cells of teleosts contain **dopa** and **5-hydroxytryptamine** (Serotonin).
39. The **ultimo-branchial** gland originates from the pharyngeal epithelium of the last or **ultimate gill pouch**.
40. The **endocrine pancreas** is present in fish as **islet of Langerhans** or brockman bodies.

13

Fish Population Dynamics and Stock Assessment

1. **B/R** = Biomass per recruit.
2. **CPUE** = Catch Per Unit Effort.
3. **E_{max}** = Exploitation level which maximizes Y/R.
4. **F** = Fishing Effort.
5. **F** = Instantaneous rate of fishing mortality.
6. **F_{max}** = Fishing Mortality generating maximum yield per recruit.
7. **F_{MSY}** = Fishing effort generating MSY.
8. **H** = natural mortality factor in Jone's length based cohort analysis.
9. **K** = Curvature parameter of VBGF.
10. Ln = $\log_e$, logarithm of base e ;Neperian logarithm.
11. Log = logarithm with base 10.
12. **MEY** = Maximum Economic Yield.
13. **R** = Recruitments.
14. **T_{max}** = longevity
15. **T_{min}** = youngest calculated age of an animal.
16. **T_c** = Age at first capture.
17. **TL** = Total length.
18. **VBGF** = Von Bertalanffy Growth Function.
19. **W_∞** = Asymptotic weight.
20. **Z** = Instantaneous rate of total mortality.
21. **Integrated method of Pauly** (1983) can be followed to calculating the **age** and **growth** of fishes.
22. **"b"** values of length weight relationship of sexes and juveniles should be tested by **Anlysis of Covariance** (Snedecor and Cochran, 1967).

23. Relative condition (Kn) of the fish can be calculated by using the equation $kn = \left\{ \frac{W}{w} \right\}$.
24. Gulland and Holt plot, **K=-b; L_∞= -a/b.**
25. Gulland and Holt plot equation reasonable only for **small values of Δt.**
26. **Ford and Walford plot** was introduced in 1933 and 1946 by without calculation of L_∞ (estimated **graphically**) and K values respectively.
27. The input data for Ford and Walford plot are **L (t) as "X" and L (t+Δt) as "Y".**
28. The input data for Chapmans method are **L (t) as "X" and L (t+Δt) -L (t) as "Y".**
29. The methods of Chapman and Gulland and Holt plot are based on the constant time interval of Δt.
30. **{L_{max}/ 0.95} = L_∞**
31. L_{max} is the **length of largest fish** reported from a well sampled stock.
32. From Bagenals' Least square method **L_∞ = {a/(1-b)}.**
33. From Bagenals' Least square method t_0= {(a-$\log_e L_\infty$)/(-b)}.
34. **M/K** is **inversely** proportional to **L_m/L_∞.**
35. The tropical fish have **higher K** values compared to cold water fishes.
36. In short lived species, particularly for tropical fishes k values are **directly proportional** to M.
37. The parameter **'ts'** is called as summer point and it takes value from **0 and 1.**
38. The parameter **'tw'** is called as winter point
39. **Mortality parameters** are useful in the estimation of yield per recruit in fishes.
40. **Z = F + M.**
41. Exponential equation
42. Annual survival rate is denoted by **'S'.**
43. $S=e^{-z}$
44. S=Nt/NO
45. Z=-ln(S)
46. Z=-log e^s
47. The proportion of the population that does not survive is known as **Annual mortality** rate.

48. **A=1-S**
49. Z can be estimated by various methods, namely by **age composition method**, by **CPUE** and by **growth parameters and mean size in the catch**.
50. **Heinchke's** method is the oldest method could be applied for **short live fishes**.
51. **Jackson method** is used for estimation of the **two adjacent age groups** in a given year class.
52. **Cushing method** can be applied for the **incomplete age composition** data for the availed fish stock.
53. Powell-Wetherall method is suited for situations where little or nothing is known about the fish stocks (L_∞=-a/b ; Z=K).
54. Natural mortality is denoted by the 'M'.
55. Fishes with **low values of K** values will **have low** values of M.
56. Z=M+qf
57. F=q*f
58. **M cannot be negative**.
59. According to **Rithter and Efanov** (1976), fish with high natural mortality mature early in life and compensates the high M by starting to reproduce earlier.
60. **E=F/Z** {Exploitation ratio}
61. **U=F/Z*(1-e^{-z})** {Exploitation rate}
62. Gulland equation for estimation of potential yield: **Py=M*0.5*Bv**.
63. Bv stands for virgin stock.
64. Ricker equation for MSY={(rm*B∞)/(4)}
65. Intrinsic rate of increase: **rm=0.025*$W^{-0.26}$**
66. Combined equation for the estimation of potential yield given by Ricker and Bluewiesset*et. al.*, 1978; Py=2.3*$W^{-0.26}$*Bv
67. Cadima's formula: MSY= 0.5*(Y+M*B)
68. MSY= **-0.25 a^2/b** (Schaefer model)
69. MSY= **-(1/d)*exp.(C-1)** (Fox model)
70. FMSY= **-0.5* a/b** (Schaefer model)
71. FMSY= **-1/d** (Fox model)
72. Fishing effort is the product of the **amount of gear in use** times the duration of the fishing activity.

73. **CPUE** = yield/effort
74. The fundamental objective of any responsible fishing operation is to give **maximum return** to the fisherman with **minimum efforts on the fish populations** and the environment.
75. Fishing selectivity is the **ability to target** and capture fish by species, size or sex during harvesting operations.
76. **Bell** shaped curve for **gill net**.
77. **Sigmoid** shaped curve for **trawl net**.
78. **Wedging** is the process of fish held tight **around the body** by a mesh.
79. **Tangling** is the process of fish caught in the net by **teeth, maxillaries** or other projections.
80. **VPA** stands for Virtual population analysis.
81. The word virtual was introduced by the Fry in 1949.
82. A **cohort** is a batch of fish all of approximately the **same age** and belonging to the **same stock**.
83. **Tris** the minimum age at which the fish can enter the fishery.
84. Tc is the age at **first capture** which marks the beginning of exploitation phase.
85. Tc is dependent on the **mesh size**.
86. The main **objective of the application of the surplus production** models is to detect the **optimum level of effort**.
87. The maximum surplus production is called as **MSY**.
88. MSY can be estimated by **Schaefer and Fox models**.
89. The data requirement for the Schaefer model is **catch and effort** data.
90. Y/F=a+b(Schaefer model)
91. Ln (Y/F) = c+d*f or Y/F = exp. c+d*f (Fox model)
92. Y/F = q.B
93. BV = a/q (Schaefer model)
94. BV = exp. c/q (Fox model)
95. Fox model seems to be more realistic than Schaefer model when a fishery undergoes transition from **traditional to mechanised fleets**.
96. Future yields and stock biomass levels can be predicted by means of **mathematical models**.
97. Yield per recruitment model is called as analytical model proposed by **Beverton and Holt**.

98. Y/R model principle = **Steady state model**.
99. **Holistic models** = Swept area method and Surplus production model.
100. The tail end of the trawl is called as **cod end**.
101. The swept area 'a' can be estimated by **a=v.t.hX2**
102. Computer packages for **stock assessment** studies were developed exclusively for tropical waters by **FAO and ICLARM** during the year 1987 and 1988.
103. Computer packages for stock assessment studies mainly based on the **length data**.
104. **ELEFAN system** – Electronic Length Frequency Analysis developed by **ICLARM**.
105. There **are 5 ELEFAN** system are present.
106. **ELEFAN I** was developed by **Pauly and David** (1987).
107. **LFSA** – Length based Fish Stock Assessment was developed by **Sparre** during 1987.
108. FiSAT stands for FAO-ICLARM Assessment Tools.
109. FiSAT = ELEFAN developed by ICLARM + LFSA developed by FAO.
110. File, Assess, Support and Utilities are the main **four basic** routines of FiSAT.
111. POPDYN developed by **FAO in 1994**.

Aquatic Animal Health Management

14

Fish and Shellfish Pathology

1. In GAS normal adaption done on **3 stages**.
2. In GAS alarm reaction is an **physical response**.
3. **Resistance stage** adaptation achieved under homeostasis.
4. In **exaust** - unable to achieved homeostasis.
5. Study of disease and their causative agent is called as **pathology**.
6. *Aeromonas salmonicida* is an **obligate** pathogen.
7. *Aeromonas hydrophilia* is an **opportunistic** pathogen.
8. Inflammation occur due to **stress**.
9. 5 signs in inflammation are calor, ruber, tumour, dolore, et function leaso.
10. Inflammation response will occur following the release of **pharmacodynamic amine**.
11. **Acute** inflammation **very sharp** and cure with in short time.
12. Resolution & exudation are **reversible** but **necrosis** is **not** reversible.
13. **Liquefactive** necrosis is done by the **enzyme digestion**.
14. **Coagulative** necrosis is due to **loss of blood supply**.
15. **Soupy fat** consistency present fat necrosis.
16. **Pyknosis** is known as **shrunken** & very dark nucleus.
17. In **karyorhexis**, rupture of nuclear membrane & fragmentation of chromatine are occurred.
18. In **Karyolysis**, nucleic acids are hydrolyzed.
19. Massive inflammation of granulation tissue known as **granuloma**.
20. Cuticle made up of **mucopolysaccharides** which have 1 micron thickness
21. In cuticle layer, **immunoglobulins, lysosome, free faty** acids are present
22. Epidermis is made up of fibrous **malphigian cells**.
23. Mucous cells also known as **coblet cell**. it is present in **middle** layer of epidermis.

24. **Club cell** have round shape. it is present in lower and middle layer of epidermis.
25. Dermis composed of two layers. they are stratum **compactum**, stratum **spongiosum**.
26. Stratum compactum is made up of dense network of **colagenous matrix**.
27. Stratum spongiosum is made up of **loss network of collagen**.
28. **Hypertrophy** means increase in **cell size**.
29. **Secondary gill filaments** act as a primary site of gas exchange
30. **Piller** cells give support to the secondary gill lamellae
31. **Lamellar oedema** - fluid accumulation in the gills
32. Lamellar hyperplasia- increase number of cells due to migration of **malphigian cells**.
33. Lamellar fusion – fusion of lamellae, its **irreversible**.
34. Haemopoitic tissue located in the stroma of the spleen, interstitum of the kidney, lymphoid organ.
35. Melanomacrophage centre only present in **teleost haemopoitic tissue**.
36. Main elements is spleen are ellipsoid pulp, **melanomacrophage**.
37. T cell mature in **thymus**.
38. **Reduction** in total mass of haemoglobin is known as **anaemia**.
39. **Haemorrhegicanaemia** is due to loss of blood.
40. **Haemolytic** anaemia is due to **erythrocyte destruction**.
41. **Haemo plastic** anaemia is due to nutritional deficiency.
42. Increase in production of white blood cell is known as **leukanaemia**.
43. Pathlogy in heart **odema & myocardial necrosis**.
44. Rhabdo virus primarily affect the **circulatory system**.
45. Entric red mouth disease is caused by ***Yersina ruckeri***.
46. Teleost liver lake of fixed **kupffer cell**.
47. In **focal necrosis** small area of liver get damage.
48. In **confluent necrosis** large area of liver get damage.
49. Hepatic carcinoma is caused by ***Aspergilus flavus***.
50. In pancreas endocrine secrete **glucogon & insulin**.
51. Acinar necrosis mostly occure in **salmon & trout**.
52. Uncontroled production of acinar cell is known as **neoplasia**.

53. Furenculosis is caused by ***A. salmonocida***.
54. Bacterial haemorrhegic septicemia is caused by ***Pseudomonas***.
55. Columnaris is caused by ***Flexibacterium columnaris***.
56. Salt water colunmnaris is caused by ***F.maritimus***.
57. Bacterial kidney disease is caused by ***Renibacterium salmoninarum***.
58. White spot disease in fish is caused by ***Icthyophthirius multifilis***.
59. Whirling disease is caused by the ***Myxosoma cerebralis***.
60. Intestinal microsporidosis is caused by the **glugeastephani**.
61. Gill rot is caused by ***Branchiomyces* sp**.
62. The EUS was first reported in **Australia in 1972**.
63. The EUS locally called as **'webakkudes'**.
64. The EUS was first noticed in **india in may1988** in fishes.
65. **CIFAX** chemical is **yellowish brown** in colour.
66. The required amount of amount of **CIFAX is 0.01mg/ l**.
67. **Furazolidon** is a drug used to control the **furunculosis**.
68. **Chealated copper and simazine** is used to control the algal.
69. **Rotenone** is a fish toxin.
70. To remove the turbidity **filter alum** is used.
71. Gypsum used to decrease the **PH**.
72. In crustacean **haemocytes** and **hyaline** cells involved in phagocytosis activity.
73. **Semi granular cell** involved in active encapsulation.
74. **Granular cell** involved in strorage and release of **prophenoloxidase**.
75. **Transglutaminase** involved in clotting and coagulating reaction in shrimp.
76. **Lectin** present in the **haemolymph** of the invertebraete.
77. Oncomiracidia is a larvae of **monogenean**.
78. Gyrodactylids are **viviparous**.
79. **Miracidium** is lavae of digenean.
80. **Coracidium** is a larvae ofcestodes.
81. Acanthocephalan need **one invertebrate host** for complete life cycle.
82. Larvae of copepode – **naupilus**.
83. Adult male copepods are **non parasites**.

84. Cocoon are laid by **leaches**.
85. Velvet disease is caused by **oodinium**.
86. Costiosis is caused by ***ichthyopodasp***.
87. White spot disease is caused by ***I.multifilus***.
88. Neon tetra disease is caused by **plistophora**.
89. Guppy killer disease Is caused by **parasitic ciliated protozoan**.
90. Hole in the disease is caused by **Hexamita**.
91. Dactlogyrus, gyrodactylus is **monogenean** parasites.
92. To kill the monogenean, **paraziquantel** bath are used .
93. Fish louse is controlled by **organo phosphate**.
94. Furunculosis has successful vaccine.
95. Hirta disease is caused by ***A. salmonicida***.
96. Virous has size ranging from **18 - 300 nm**.
97. IPNV belonging to the **Birnaviridae**.
98. Cotton wool disease is caused by **Saprolegnia**.
99. OIE- office internatonal des epizotics established in **1924**.
100. OIE become world organization of animal health in **2003**.
101. Nutritional disease is described by **Seniesko**.
102. Amino acid deficiency leads to **impairment of growth**.
103. Dorsal fin erosion is due to **lysine** deficiency.
104. Spinal deformities is associated with - **Tryptophan**.
105. Excess carbohydrate leads to **Haepatocytes Denaturation**.

Aquatic Environment Management

15

Meteorology, Climatology and Geography

1. Meteorology is the branch of science that deals with the **study of the atmosphere**.
2. The scientific study of the interactions between living organisms and their atmospheric environment is called as **Biometeorology**.
3. 75% of the mass of atmosphere is in the **troposphere**.
4. The ozone layer present in **stratosphere**.
5. **Exosphere** gradually merges into interplanetary space.
6. The concentration of ozone occurs between 20 and 50 Km with the maximum around 25 km which is referred as **ozonosphere**.
7. Chromospheres – the layer which has the chemical activity predominant between 20 and 100 km.
8. Atmospheric composition varies above 80-100 km which is called as Heterosphere.
9. Heliosphere – Molecular oxygen is seen been between 200 and 1000 km.
10. Ionosphere – above 10000 km, hydrogen atoms are in an ionized state.
11. The earth's magnetic field extends outwards into space to nearly ten earth radii called as **magnetosphere**.
12. Short term variation in the atmosphere at a given place is called as **Weather**.
13. The condition of the atmosphere over a long period of time over a large area is called as **climate**.
14. Conduction – **heat transfer between solids**.
15. **Convection** – heat transfer between liquids.
16. **Radiation** – heat transfer without the involvement of the physical substance.

17. **Advection** – the process of horizontal transfer of heat by winds.
18. **Insolation** – Incoming Solar Radiation.
19. Ratio of diffusely reflected radiation to the incident radiation – **Albedo**.
20. A line connecting the places having highest average temperature is known as **heat equator**.
21. The highest temperature recorded in Tripol of North Africa (136 °C).
22. The actual decrease in temperature with elevation is called **Actual Lapse Rate**.
23. The average rate of temperature decrease with the elevation is called as Normal Lapse Rate.
24. The total volume of water in the atmosphere is about $1.3X10^{13}$.
25. Ratio of the **actual vapor pressure to the saturation vapor pressure** at a given air temperature – Relative humidity.
26. The difference between the actual temperature and to the dew point is called as **dew point depression**.
27. 1783 – De Saussure used Hair hygrometer to measure the moisture of the air.
28. The hygrometer may be transformed into a self-recording instrument which is called as hygrograph.
29. **Psychrometer** – widely used instrument for measuring humidity.
30. Sleet = Rain + snow.
31. Ice pellets = 0.5 to 5.0 cm.
32. Pressure is measured by a **barometer**.
33. Isobars are the lines joining the points **of equal pressure**.
34. The change in pressure with horizontal distance is called **pressure gradient**.
35. Rain bearing clouds are categorized as **nimbus**.
36. Clouds with fibrous appearance – **cirriform clouds**.
37. CCN – cloud condensation nuclei.
38. Cumulonimbus clouds often give rise to **squalls**.
39. Diameter of the cyclone ranges from **200 - 2000 km**.
40. WMO – world Meterological organization.
41. The earth is an oblate **spheroid**.
42. Core is located at the **Earth's center**.

43. The thickness of mantle is **2900 Km** (which comprises 83% of the Earth's volume).
44. The crust floats on **top of the mantle**.
45. Crust = Basalt (Oceanic crust) + Granitic (Continental crust).
46. The top layer of the upper mantle is called **Asthenosphere**.
47. The **lithosphere** is a layer that includes the crust and upper most portion of the asthenosphere.
48. **Longitude** is an important factor in determining time in **all parts of the world**.
49. The linear distance between two given longitude is **maximum at the equator** and is reduced to zero at the poles.
50. Hydrometer is used to measure **moisture**.
51. Smog is a **polluted fog**.
52. The regular decrease in temperature with altitude is called **vertical temperature gradients**.
53. Precipitation = Bergeron process + subsequent growth by coalescence.
54. Oceans are called as **heat reservoirs**.
55. Diameter of ice pellets: less than **5 mm**.
56. Diameter of snow pellets: less than **2.5 mm**.
57. Hailstones are small balls of chunks having 5 - 75 mm of diameter.
58. India gets **80% of annual precipitation** from monsoon.
59. Water in the atmosphere exists mainly as an invisible gas and water vapour.
60. Green house gases play a major role in Green house effect and global warming.
61. **Condensation** is an important aspect of weather.
62. Vapour to ice: **Deposition**.
63. Vapour to liquid: **Condensation**.
64. Liquid to vapour: **Evaporation**.
65. Ice to vapour: **Sublimation**.
66. Mixing ratio is the mass of water vapour in a unit of dry air
67. Partial pressure is usually expressed as **millibars/ inches of mercury**.
68. Dew point is below freezing is referred as **frost point**.
69. An electrical hygrometer is used in **Radio Sonde**.

70. The satellites are able to detect the humidity with troposphere.
71. The process by which objects become covered with small water droplets are known as **guttation**.
72. Glazed frost is called as **Silver frost**.
73. Freezing of super cooled water droplets are called as **Rime**.
74. Condensation trails – Contrails
75. When air moves across a much warmer water surface a kind of fog is formed called as steam fog.
76. Atmosphere has 5% of average water vapour.
77. Water vapour mainly observed in radiation.
78. The mass of water vapour in a unit of dry air is called as **mixing ratio**.
79. The dew point below freezing is referred as **frost point**.
80. The electrically changed position of atmosphere is known as **Ionosphere**.
81. Auroras observed most frequently of 20° and 30° latitude from the geomagnetic poles.
82. The outer most region of the atmosphere is called as magnetosphere.
83. Relatively mixed gases present in **homosphere layer**.
84. Various amount of gases present in **heterosphere layer**.
85. CFC gas release – **chlorine gas**.
86. Coldest point in the atmosphere is **mesopause**.
87. Ozone layer found in **stratosphere layer**.
88. Temperature decrease is found in the troposphere layer.
89. **Density particle** is very low in exosphere layer.
90. The condition of temperature constant and then it increases was found in the layer called as stratosphere.
91. Water vapour present in stratosphere layer.
92. The average temperature of troposphere is about 6.5°C/ km.
93. Hydrogen gas present in exosphere layer.
94. Temperature of thermosphere is high as 1100°C.
95. In exosphere, the particles escape through gravitational pull on the earth.
96. Troposphere is a zone of dense, turbulent and air with abundant water vapour and oxygen.
97. Meteorology is study of weather change.
98. Interactions between living organisms and atmospheric environment are called as biometeorology.

99. **Aeronomy** – investigates both the chemical and physical changes in atmosphere.
100. The mass of atmosphere – 5.6 X 10^{14} tonnes.
101. Meteorology pertaining to sea and ocean is called as Marine meteorology.
102. Oxygen is a highly reactive gas that supports aerobic respiration.
103. Insolation – Incoming Solar radiation.
104. Insolation is commonly expressed in the units of watts/m^2 or Calories/cm^2/min or Langley/min.
105. Forms of precipitation – Rain, Snow, Sleet, Dew.
106. Drizzle – **less than 0.5 mm dia**.
107. Rain drops – **0.05 to 0.06 cm in dia**.
108. Ice pellets or Sleet – less than 5 mm in dia.
109. Snow pellets – **2 to 5 mm** in dia.
110. Snow grains – less than 1mm in dia.
111. Hailstones (small balls or chunks of ice) – less than 5 to 75mm in dia.
112. Precipitation = Bergeron + Coalescence process.
113. The percentage of radiation reflected is called as **Albedo**.
114. Beaufort scale – used to state the strength of wind.
115. Cup Anemometer – measures the **speed of wind**.
116. Sling Psychrometer – measures **the humidity**.
117. PicheEvaporimeter – measures evaporation rate of the water in atmosphere.
118. **Thermograph** – mechanical device used to measure the temperature variation.
119. Bimetal strip (a kind of thermometer) – works on the principle of a differential expansion.
120. Sunshine recorder (a kind of recorder) – records the sunrise and sun set time.
121. Pyranometer – used to measure daily cycle of incoming short wave radiation to ground surface.
122. Rain gauge – measures the depth of accumulated precipitation.
123. Hytherograph – Hydrograph + Thermograph.
124. Hydrograph – record humidity.
125. Barograph – measures the changes in the atmospheric pressure.

126. **Anemograph** – measure the **direction** and the **speed** of the wind.
127. Wind wane – measure the **direction of the wind**.
128. Barometer – measure **atmospheric pressure**.
129. Absolute humidity – amount of water vapour actually present in the given volume of air.
130. Relative humidity – amount of water vapour actually present in the given volume of air at a particular temperature to the amount of water vapour required to saturate the same temperature.
131. **Pie graphs** also called as circular, coin or sector graphs.
132. Climate of a region can be expressed by simple rainfall and temperature – Climatograms
133. Scale – relationship between a distance measured on the map and true distance on the ground.
134. Cadastral map – individual landed property and land registration.
135. Wall map – small scale map representing relief, climate, vegetation types, soil types, minerals, roads, railways, etc.
136. Isopleths – lines that connect places of equal value.
137. Choropleth maps – shows civic divisions.
138. Dot maps – shows method of distribution.
139. Gradient winds – height of 600 m that blows parallel to the isobars.
140. Geotropic wind – occurs from the balance between the pressure gradient and coriolis force.
141. The study of ocean is called as **oceanography**.
142. Oceanography comes from the **Greek words**: Oceanus – ocean and Graphos – study.
143. Ring shaped reefs enclosing land lesslagoon is called **as Atolls**.
144. An elongated reef separated from the land mass by some distance is termed **as barrier reef**.
145. Extension of the sea or ocean into the land mass, being completely land locked on 33 sides are known as **Bay**.
146. Narrow strip of ocean / sea which enters into the land mass is called as **Gulf**.
147. Narrow strip of water body connecting seas and oceans are known as **Strait**.
148. Narrow strip of land mass which plunges into the sea and oceans being abounded by oceanic water on all 3 sides are called **as Cape**.

149. Representations of depth contours of the ocean floor is called as **Bathymetric charts**.
150. Narrow steep walled ocean inlet is called as **Fjord**.
151. The line along which air masses of differing characteristics meet is called as **Frontal system**.
152. Flat-topped sea mount is known as **Guyot**.
153. The circular flow of oceanic circulation is called as **Gyre**.
154. The zone in the ocean in which salinity rapidly changes is termed as **Halocline**.
155. The contour line representing the similar depth in the bathymetric chart is defined as **Isobaths**.
156. The boundary where the land and water meets is defined as **Shore line**.

16

Limnology

1. The term limnology is derived from **Greek word**.
2. Limne means **lake**.
3. The term limnology was coined by Francois-Alponse forel.
4. August Thienemann and EinarNaumann co-founded the international society of limnology.
5. Welch 1935 described about biological productivity.
6. **Epheirology** is defined as branch of science deals with terrestrial habitats.
7. Peter Erasmus Muller is credited with laying the foundation stone of limnological study.
8. Anton Fritsch could be considered as the Pioneer in Lacustrine limnology.
9. F.Simony (1850) is regarded sometimes as the founder of limnology for his discovery of thermal stratification.
10. Junge and Forbes who were the first to treat the native waters as microcosm.
11. Gaarder and Gran made a pioneering attempts measuring the photoautotrophic production.
12. Direct method of carbon assimilation – steemann Nielsen (1952).
13. Energy transport along the food chain – lindeman (1942).
14. New direction to limnology – cook (1977).
15. Deep water fauna of lake Michigan – Stimson.
16. Limnoplankton – **plankton of lakes**.
17. Heleoplankton – plankton of **ponds**.
18. Potamoplanlton – plankton of **rivers**.
19. Standing waters – **lentic** waters.
20. Flowing waters – **lotic** waters.

21. **Aestival pond** – waters persists in these ponds throughout the season but, it freezes in winter.
22. Lake Baikal – excess of 400m to 1620m **deepest lake**.
23. Caspian Sea – 436400 **great salt lake**.
24. The estimated total of these large lakes 179000 km2 constitute 75% of the total inland surface water of the world.
25. Carpenter 1928 formulated the true difference between lake and pond according to the depth.
26. **Fluvial lake** – it is formed by the **river** activity.
27. **Aeolian lakes** – formed by the **wind activity** in arid regions.
28. Young lakes are called as **oligotrophic lakes**.
29. Shallow and phosphorus lakes are called as **eutrophic lakes**.
30. Humus rich soil is called as **Eutrophic**.
31. Dystrophic lake – **rich in sallow in nature**.
32. Dal lake – Himachal Pradesh.
33. **Roopkund Lake** – known for shallow waters.
34. **Pushkarlake** – artificial lake in Rajasthan.
35. Osman sagar lake – popularly known as **Gandhipet**.
36. Bathymetry – contour map.
37. Pure water weighs about 62.4 lb. per cu. Ft at 4°C.
38. Water is virtually incompressible.
39. The coefficient of compressibility is given for atmosphere 52.5×10^{-6} at 0 °C for 1 25 atmospheres.
40. The quantity of dissolved solids for inland waters is usually below **1 g/l**.
41. The density difference is due to chemical factors is not more than 0.85 g/l.
42. Maximum density of freshwater is **at 4°C and** it becomes less dense when the temperature decreases from 4°C to freezing point.
43. Maximum density of seawater **is 0°C**.
44. The total amount of dissolved substances in freshwater is less than that in seawater.
45. **Evaporation increases the** density by concentrating the dissolved materials.

46. The bottom water of deep lakes cannot be any colder than water at its density maximum, or about 4°C.
47. Sea water freezes at **-1.91°C**.
48. Pressure does not cause any significant change in **viscosity**.
49. **Buoyancy** is the direct outcome of density.
50. Buoyancy of an object is equal to the **weight of the water** of displaces.
51. The greater the density, the greater the buoyant force; the denser the water, the floating object will ride higher in the water.
52. Ship passing from freshwater into seawater rises little higher.
53. The principal forms of movements of water are waves, currents and seiches.
54. Waves are produced by **winds**.
55. Stenenson (1934) formulated a formula for computing the maximum height of wave in small bodies of water. .
56. The water particle moves up and down but no horizontal movement of water is called as waves of **oscillation**.
57. Definite forward movement of water is a type of wave called as **waves of translation**.
58. Wave action may exert an influence to a depth of **182m**.
59. Currents in lakes: Vertical; horizontal and returning currents.
60. Oscillations of the water level under certain circumstances are called as **seiches**.
61. Surface tension of water is **7.28 X 10^{-3}N /m** for pure water at **20°C**.
62. 7.28 X 10^{-3}N/m = 72.8 dyne/cm.
63. Organisms related to the surface film are known as **neuston**.
64. Tropical lakes – Surface temperature is always maintained at **above 4°C**.
65. Temperate lakes – Surface temperature vary **above and below** 4°C.
66. Polar lakes – Surface temperature is **never goes** above 4°C.
67. Water has the greatest specific heat of all substances, except **liquid hydrogen and lithium** at high temperatures.
68. The specific heat of water is **1**.
69. The thermal conductivity of the water is **very low**.
70. Co-efficient of expansion – **1.125**.
71. Thermocline layer is called as **metalimnion**.

72. Dichothermy – Summer stratification with minimum temperature at some intervening level.
73. Mesothermy – maximum temperature at some intervening level.
74. Poikilothermy – Both maximum and minimum temperature in some intervening layer.
75. Pure water bodies appear nearly black as they absorb all light components of the **spectrum**.
76. CDOM – Colored Dissolved Organic Matter.
77. Degree of opaqueness developed in water by means of suspended water is known as **turbidity**.
78. The solubility of **gases in water decreases** with **increasing temperature** and **decrease** of **pressure**.
79. The total solubility of gas is expressed by **Henry's law**.
80. The concentration of a saturated solution of gas is proportional to the pressure at which the gas is supplied (Henry law: $C = Kp$).
81. **Carbon-dioxide** is the **second largest** decomposition product, constituting 3 to 30 percent of the total gas evolved.
82. Methane is also called as **marsh gas**.
83. Methane bacteria are **obligate anaerobes**.
84. Hydrogen sulfide is poisonous to aerobic organisms because it inactivates the enzyme **cytochrome oxidase**.
85. Nitrogen has a **low solubility** in water.
86. Rain water contains **30 to 40 ppm** of dissolved solids.
87. The solubility of solid substances is strongly dependent on **pH** and **redox potential** in the water.
88. **Carbonate** is the principal anion in most fresh waters.
89. Carbonate occurs as bicarbonate ion with calcium in water (Calcite and aragonite).
90. Inorganic form of nitrogen is Nitrate, Nitrite and Ammonia.
91. Free phosphorous does not occur in nature, but in the form of phosphates it is abundant.
92. Soluble inorganic phosphate – **Orthophosphate and Polyphosphate**.
93. Silicon does not occur in nature as a free element.
94. Dissolved silica remains as H_2SiO_4.

95. Anorthite ($CaAl_2Si_2O_8$) is a common member of the fledspar group of silicates.
96. Gypsum ($CaSo_{4.}2H_2O$).
97. Anhydrite ($CaSo_4$).
98. **Epsom salt** ($Mg\ So_4.7H_2O$)
99. Magnesium carbonate is called as **Magnetite**.
100. The common water soluble mineral is halite/ **NaCl**.
101. Slatterns having concentration of sea water with preponderance of NaCl.
102. Saline lakes having **Na_2SO_4** in water.
103. Soda lakes characterized by $NaHCO_3$ and Na_2CO_3 (having luxuriant growth of blue green algae).
104. Molecular chloride is a heavy **yellow lethal gas**.
105. In oligotrophic lakes, the volume of the **hypolimnion** is **greater** than the volume of epiliminion.
106. A rise of 1 °C increases the rate of metabolism about **10 percent**.
107. Excess nitrogen cause - **gas disease** in fishes.
108. Calcium is required by all green plants except some of the lower algae.
109. **Food production** – process of energy transformation.
110. Primary production is highly dependent on **light energy**.

17

Aquatic Pollution

1. F_e produce **inky taste.**
2. Phenol produce **bitter taste.**
3. Anaebena produce strong **grassy odour.**
4. A protozoan **dinobryon** imparts **fishy odour** to the water.
5. **Phosphorus** compound produce wormy smell.
6. H_2S produce **rotten egg** or putrid smell.
7. Humus produce **earthy odour.**
8. Sewage contain **99% of water & 1% solids.**
9. Sewage contain **70% organic** & **30% of inorganic** in nature.
10. In sewage organic fraction contain **60% of protiens** & **20% of carbohydrate &10% fat.**
11. In sewage total suspended solids **200-300 ppm**, BOD **200 - 250 ppm**, COD **-350 = 450 ppm.**
12. Shannon & Wiener diversity index is H=(epi) log2 pi
13. In sewage treatment solid are separated from liquid by **physical process.** then liquid is purified by **biological process.**
14. Preliminary treatment is used to remove the **larger solids & floatation materials.**
15. Primary treatment can be remove **70% solids & 50% of the BOD.**
16. Secondary treatment is done by the **micriorganisms**
17. The aim of tertiary treatment is **"polishing"** the secondarily treated water
18. A commonly used oxidant in COD assay is $\mathbf{K_2cr_2O_7}$.
19. Oxygen consuming potential of cellulose is **not measured in the BOD assay**
20. Oxygen consuming potential of cellulose is **measured in COD assay**
21. Red tide is caused by ***Karenia brevis***

22. **DDT** – dichloro diphenyl trichloroethane is an **insecticide**
23. DE- **dichloro diphenyl ethane**
24. DD&DE are derived from **DDT**
25. HCH **-hexachloro cyclohexane**
26. Most toxic dioxin is **2, 3, 7, 8 - TCDD** (tetra chlorodibenzo-p-dioxin)
27. Minamata disease is caused by **mercury**
28. Heavy metals have atomic weight from **63 - 200**
29. The first incidence of mercury poisoning occurred in **Japan at 1950s**
30. **Tobaco smoke** is the primary source of **cadmium**
31. ***itai-itai*** disease is caused by the primary source of cadmium
32. Manufacturing of glass will produce **arsenic**
33. **Lead** are insoluble in water
34. **Tetraethyl lead** are **more toxic** than inorganic lead
35. Lead poisoning result in kidney disease **"nephrites"**
36. **SDS** -sodium dodecyl sulphate
37. Phytoremediation is relatively new ,coined in 1991
38. Alpha particles **proton**
39. Betta particles **electron**
40. The gamma radiation produce energy level change of **nucleus in the atoms**
41. Old units for the radiation **curie, rad, rem**
42. New units for radiation **bequrel , gray, Sievert**
43. **Nuclei of nitrogen react with cosmic rays** and produce C_{14}
44. Oxygen react with cosmic rays produce **tritium**
45. Iodine 131 will affect the **thyroid**
46. Strontium 90 will affect the **bone**
47. Manganese 54 will affect the **liver**
48. The water (prevention &control of pollution) act-**1974**
49. The water (prevention & control of pollution) cess act **1977**
50. The air (prevention & control of pollution) act **1981**
51. The public liability insurance act **1981**
52. EIA (environmental impact assessment notification)-**1994**
53. The water area from low tide line to 12 nautical mile on the seaward side is comes under the CRZ 4

54. Half life of **endofuran** is **50 days**
55. Risk = toxicity & exposure
56. LD_{50} value measured in the unit of **mg\ kg** and **ppm**
57. LC_{50} is measured in the unit of **mg\L & ppm** some times **mg\m^3**
58. DO measured **mg\ L & ppm**
59. NaCl – **Dominant in hydrosphere**.
60. **Biofilm** – Communities of micro-organisms attached to a surface.
61. WHO recommends the total consumption of methyl mercury should not exceed **0.2 mg per week**.
62. Composition of sewage – **99% of water + 1% of solids**.
63. **Shannon & Weiner's diversity index** is one of the methods for determining biological indices of organic pollution.
64. Too much of phosphorous results in **algal blooms**.
65. Calcium is essential for **plant growth**.
66. **Magnesium** is the central atom in every chlorophyll molecule.
67. **Chlorine** is essential for osmosis and ionic balance.
68. **Molybdenum** is essential for **nitrogen metabolism**.
69. Boron is essential for calcium utilization, nucleic acid synthesis and membrane integrity.
70. Manganese, Zinc and Copper is essential for **enzyme activation**.
71. Sediment composition = Quartz, feldspar and carbonate-rich compounds.

Fish Processing Technology

18

Freezing Technology

1. Carotenoid act as **antioxidant**
2. The energy source for ATP generation in the light muscle is **glycogen**
3. Dark muscle contain much **more mitochondria** than the light muscle
4. Phospholipid also called as **structural lipid**
5. Light muscle mostly generating energy by the **anaerobic metabolism**
6. The **triglyceride** are known as the **depot fat**
7. Cod contain less than **1 % lipid**
8. Lean fish contain **6% of the cholesterol** of the total lipid
9. Squalene also known as **diacetyl – alkyl - glycerol**
10. Shark liver oil contain minimum 80 % of the lipid as **un saponifiable substances**
11. In marine fish **fatty acid constitute** only around 2% of the lipid
12. **Structural protein** also known as **miofibrilar protein**. it will soluble in high ionic strength solution
13. Sarcoplasmic protein soluble in **natural solution**
14. Elasmobranch contain **10% collagen**
15. **NPN**- fraction constitute from **9-18 %** of the total lipid nitrogen in teleost
16. The highest amount of **TMAO** found in **elasmobranches and squid**
17. The **flat fish** and **pelagic fish** have least amount of TMAO
18. The main component of NPN fraction is **creatine**
19. Salt water fish content high content of **iodine**
20. TMA has - **fishy smell**
21. **Octopine** is the end product from the **anaerobic** metabolism of **cephalopod**
22. In **anaerobic condition** only **2 moles** of ATP produced

23. In **aerobic** condition **36 moles** of ATP produced
24. The muscle toughness and PH have **inverse relationship**
25. ATP also act as a **plasticizer**
26. Rigor mortis starts **ATP** concentration below **10^{-4} M** and that of **Ca^{+} above 10^{-6} M**
27. The **Cathepsins** are hydrolytic enzyme situated in **lysosomes**
28. **Cathepsins** are involved in **ripening** of marinated fish product
29. Thermophiles grow at above **45 ^{0}C**
30. Mesophiles grows at above **25 - 37 ^{0}C**
31. Psychrotrophs will grow in the temperature **0 - 25 ^{0}C**
32. The psychrophiles have maximum growth temperature around **20 ^{0}C**
33. During the ice storage of fish **50 - 60%** of microbes will be die
34. The **tropical** fishes have **low level** of the **psychrotrophs**
35. Latent heat of fusion of ice is about **80K cal/ kg**
36. In **shelving** only **one layer of ice** was added
37. **10 - 15 cm** expanded **polystyrene** is common for **insulated box**
38. Specific heat of **frozen fish 0.4**
39. The flake ice having thickness about **2 - 3 mm**
40. Flake ice are stored in **refrigerated silo**
41. The plate ice having thickness about **8 - 15 mm**
42. Tube ice having **50 mm** dia and **10 - 12 mm thickness**
43. In CSW mixture of the sea water and ice about **1:1 to 1:2**
44. As per the **rule of the thumb** the self-life of the **0^{0} stored** fish is **double than the 5 ^{0}C stored fish**
45. As per the EIC to process the **1 kg of** fish **12 L of water** is required
46. The water used by the plant should be meet specification as given in the council directive **80/ 778/ EEC**
47. The water should not contain total chloride content is **250 mg /l** the MPN index should be **less than one**
48. The maximum permitted limit of total hardness in water **600 mg/ l as $CaCO_3$**
49. Copper content of the water should be **1mg/ l**
50. Lead should be **0.1 mg/ L**
51. Nitrate **20 mg/ l**

52. **L. monocytogens** more resistance to the **chlorine**
53. At - 5 ^{0}C frozen product will have remaining **20% of the water**
54. At – 30 ^{0}C approximately **10% water remains** unfrozen
55. **Thermal arrest period** occurred at the temperature -1.1to -5 ^{0}C
56. In thermal arrest period **55% of the water** is turned to ice
57. Variety of irregular shaped product can be frozened by using the **air blast freezer**
58. Bulk freezing can be done by using the **vertical plate freezer**
59. In liquid nitrogen freezer the compressor and condenser are **not needed**
60. Heat introduced to the frozen product is known as **thawing**
61. The air blast thawing machine should have air velocity about **6 m/ sec**
62. Dielectric thawer has thermal efficiency of about **70 %**
63. The rate of weight loss of frozen fish in cold storage is **50g/ m^2/ 24h**
64. The pigment responsible for the **pink colour** in normal cooked meat of tuna is **hemochrome**
65. Melonoldehyde is estimated by the **TBA test**
66. In lipid oxidation the **first step** is the formation of **hydrogen peroxide**
67. Lipid oxidation takes place in fishes having more than **2% of the body** weight of lipid
68. Polymer of PVD better known for **saran**
69. Polyester film has trade name as **Mylar**
70. Corrugated fiber box is made up of **fluked sheet** glued between two line
71. Type A flute contain - **35 flutes per inch**
72. Type B flute contain – **50 flutes per inch**
73. Type e flutes contain **90 flutes per inch**
74. **Shrink packaging** was introduced by cryovac company in **1948**
75. The well designed trickle filter can be removed **85 - 95 %** of the BOD
76. Tertiary treatment also known as **advanced waste treatment**
77. The principle source of Ciguatera toxin is **Gambierdiscus toxicus**

19

Fish Canning and Packaging Technology

1. Father of caning **Nicholas apart**
2. Tin canister invented by **Peter Durand**
3. Father of modern canning **Bryon Dorkin**
4. Pure food act – **1906**
5. Invention of pressure retort – **1874**
6. Double seaming machine invented in – **1890**
7. OTS can invented in – **1904**
8. The first Indian canning industry was constructed in **1911 at chaliyam,** Kerala
9. PH above 5.3 food known as – **low acid food**
10. **PH 4.5 - 5.3** – known as medium acid food
11. Acid food contain PH about **3.7 - 4.5**
12. **High acid food** contain PH about – below 3.7
13. **Lacquering** is done before cutting the tin plate
14. The term Lacquering is **British word** & **Enamel** is in **USA**
15. Acid resistant **oleoresin lacquer** are commonly used
16. Sulphur resistant lacquer are **oleo resinous C. enamels**
17. C enamel containing **zinc oxide**
18. Oleoresin's lacquer **gold** in colour
19. The ideal can composition is **98% of steel** and **2% of tin**
20. Thickness of steel plate varies from **0.19 - 0.3 mm**
21. **CMQ** - can making quality
22. **Copper and phosphorus** play in important role in **corrosion** nature of the can
23. **Phosphorus** content increase the **stiffness** of the can

24. Tin plate **deoxidized** by using the **silicon and aluminum** this process called **Hithing**
25. In roughness process high pressure water spray to the surface of the **stripes**
26. Removal of oxide film is known as **pickling** is done by using the **sulphuric acid & electrolysis**
27. In cold reduction process the thickness of the tin plate reduced to **10 fold**
28. Hot reduction also called as annealing .in that **580 - 600 ^{0}C** temperature are used
29. **Base box is the unit** of express the thickness of the tin plate. it contain **112 sheet**
30. Now the thickness expressed in **gms/ m^2**
31. A recommended D coating is **11.2/ 5.6**
32. Electrophoretic tin plate some time known as **9 layer sandwich**
33. Quality grading of tin plate known as **assorting** of tin plate
34. Thermoplastic cement - **nylon**
35. DWI- introduced in **1964** in **USA**
36. Corrosion in tin container is due to **electrochemical reaction**
37. Due to corrosion **hydrogen** gas are formed
38. Phosphorus content should be less than **0.02 %**
39. Porosity of tin coating should be minimum less than **20 micron**
40. **Bulking** is due to improper **cooling**
41. **Paneling** due to excessive **external pressure**
42. **GMP**- good manufacturing practices
43. **Deskining** is done by dip in **caustic soda**
44. Blanching also called **braining**
45. Hot blanching done for **prawn** and **vegetables**
46. Flavor enhancer – **monosodium glutamate**
47. Precooking time the fish flesh release **15 - 30 %** of water
48. **Zink chloride** used as a flux in soldering the side seam of the can body
49. Brine is the most additive in the **canned food**
50. Penetration of salt take place **3 days**
51. Oil impregnate to the fish at **18 - 20 days**
52. **Long exhausting** is **better** than the short exhausting at high temperature

53. Double seaming consist of **5 thickness of metal**
54. Aseptic packaging was introduced by **Olin ball in 1930**
55. Moist heat **121 - 129 ^{0}C**
56. Dry heat **176 - 232 ^{0}C**
57. Sterilization of air by incineration at temperature **260 - 315 ^{0}C**
58. Sturvite crystal formation – **magnesium ammonium phosphate Hexa hydrate**
59. Honey comb formation occurred in **canned tuna**
60. **Mush** formation occurred in canned **pilchard**
61. Mush- by chloromysium
62. **Curd** formation occurred in canned **mackerel and salmon**
63. **Blue discoloration** in canned crab due to **copper** content is more **than 2 mg %** (normal 0.49%)
64. TMAO at 13 mg% can cause **greening** of tuna
65. Retort pouch introduced in USA at **1948**
66. The outer layer of retort pouch is **PES at 122 micron**
67. Middle layer – **aluminum foil**
68. Inner layer – **poly propylene**
69. HBS - **hot bar sealing**
70. EVA - **ethylene vinyl acetate**
71. MRE - **meal ready to eat**
72. Basic function of packaging - **containment**
73. UPC - **universal product code**
74. Anti-blocking agent **Stearamide**
75. Anti fogging agent – **non-ionic ethoxylates**
76. Antimicrobial agent – **copper 8 quinoleate**
77. Antioxidant - **BHT**
78. Antizonants - **waxes**
79. Antioxidant also called as **aging retardant**
80. Antislip agent also called as **slip depressant**
81. Antislip agent – **colloidal silica**
82. Tefra pack – **containing 6 layer**
83. Mesophilic anaerobes – **C. sporagenes**

84. Mesophilic aerobes – **Bacillus sp**
85. Cobb's test is a **water absorbent test**
86. Blue discoloration occurred in **canned crab**
87. Black discoloration occurred in **shrimp**
88. Green discoloration occurred in **tuna**
89. Hydrostatic cooker – Pierre Carvallo in 1948.
90. First reel and spiral cooker was developed by Anderson & Born Grover in 1924.
91. Aseptic canning – **C.Olin Ball**.
92. **ULD** – Unit Load Device.
93. Bulgingon both ends – **true spoilage**.
94. No bulging but spoil – **flat sour spoilage**.
95. Containers distortion is due to **faulty operation**.
96. Honey combing occurs in **tuna meat**.
97. Struvite crystal formation: $\mathbf{MgNH_4PO_4.6H_2O}$
98. Mush – **Flabby Condition** (especially in Pilchards).
99. **Retort burn** – due to insufficient filling medium.
100. Putrefactive anaerobes – ***Clostridium sporogenes***.
101. **Yeast** – *Torulalactiscondensi*.
102. **Mould** – *Aspergilus ripens*.
103. Father of canning – **Nicholas appert**.
104. Inventor of tin canister – **peter Durand**.
105. First commercial canning factory in England – John Hall and **Bryan Dorkin** (1846).
106. **Gill espy** – Principles of heat sterilization.
107. Alfred Appleyard and Fred Hist – Can body maker.
108. Specific heat of water is **1**.
109. Antiblocking agents – **Stearamide + Polyethylene**.
110. Antifogging agent – **Glyceryl stearate**.
111. Antimicrobial agents – Algicides; Bactericides; Fungicides; Copper-8-quinoleate and N-tricholomethylthiophthalimide.
112. Antioxidant agents - BHT; BHA.
113. Antioxidant agent is also called as **aging retardants or stabilizers**.

114. Antiozonants – wax and inert plastics.
115. Antislip agents – Colloidal silica solution; co-polymers of ethylene; Maleic anhydride.
116. Antistatic agents are used to minimize **static electricity**.
117. PBA – Physical Blowing agents (N_2; CO_2).
118. CBA – Chemical Blowing agents (Volatile aliphatic hydrocarbons; hexane; methylene chloride).
119. Electrically conductive agents – **Dopants**.
120. Flame retardant agents – Polyethylene + Antimony trioxide; chlorinated paraffin.
121. Heat stabilizer agents – Barium; **Cadmium; Lead**.
122. Impact modifier agents – Acrylic polymer + PVC at 7.5 wt %.
123. Lubricants used in injection moulding are called as **release agents**.
124. Tearing resistance determines the average force in gram force **(gf/ N)**.
125. WVTR accepted unit is **1g/ 24h/ m^2**.
126. EU regulations – Plastic Directive set up in 1995.
127. SML – Specific Migration Level.
128. **Terephthalic acid** is a principle monomer in manufacture of PET Plastic.
129. **Isocyanates** are used in the manufacture of polyurethane and certain acrylates.
130. ADI – Acceptable Daily Intake.
131. TDI – Tolerable Daily Intake.
132. Pullulan is depolymerised by a number of enzaymes and the glucose monomers are subsequently mineralized produced y Aureobasidium pullulan.

20

Food Chemistry

1. **Food** is an essential part in everyday life.
2. The major biomolecules of the food which perform these functions called **nutrients**.
3. The study of various nutrients in relation to their effect upon the human body is called as **nutrition**.
4. **Major nutrients**: Carbohydrates, Lipids, Proteins, Minerals, Vitamins and water.
5. Insufficient food intake of necessary minimum amount of any nutrient leads tot state of **malnutrition**.
6. No food intake leads to **starvation**.
7. Water is not always included as nutrients, but it is essential that the diet provides sufficient water required for many functions of the body.
8. Lipids provide calories and essential fatty acids.
9. Lipids = 98% of triglycerides + 2% phospholipids.
10. Lipids carry **fat soluble vitamins**.
11. Linoleic acid and linolenic acids are needed as the precursor of **arachidonic acid**.
12. Animal fat contain or very rich in **polyunsaturated** fatty acids.
13. **Plant and fish** fat contain or very rich in polyunsaturated fatty acids.
14. The vitamins are organic **micronutrients**, required is only milligram or microgram quantities per day.
15. Fat soluble vitamins – **A, D, E, K**.
16. Water soluble vitamins – **B and C**.
17. Vitamins help to maintain organs and tissues healthy.
18. **Minerals** are simple inorganic substances.
19. **Glucose** is an important carbohydrate.
20. Carbohydrates are derivatives of **polyhydroxy aldehydes or ketones**.

21. Greek word of Carbohydrates – **SAKCHARON**.
22. **Monosaccharides** are those carbohydrates that cannot be hydrolyzed to simpler compounds.
23. Monosaccharides are subdivided into trioses, tetroses, pentoses, hexoses and heptoses depending upon the **number of the carbon atoms**.
24. Lactose is the principal sugar present in **milk**.
25. **Raffinose** and **stachyose** are two important oligosaccharides.
26. Polysaccharides – **glycogen** present in animal muscles and liver.
27. Polysaccharides – **starches and dextrin** present in plant tissues.
28. **Stereochemistry** is the study of arrangement of atoms in three dimensional space.
29. **Stereoisomers** are compounds in which the atoms are linked in the **same order** but differ in their **spatial arrangements**.
30. The carbon atom attached to four **different** atoms are linked is called as **asymmetric carbon**.
31. **Dextrorotatory** – plane polarized light towards **right** side (+ sign).
32. **Levorotatory** - plane polarized light towards **left** side (- sign).
33. **Pyranose** sugars contain a six member ring.
34. **Furanose** sugars contain a five member ring.
35. Glucose forms both a **pyranose** and **furanose** sugars in **a ring structure**.
36. Isomers formed as a result of –H and –OH on carbon atom 2, 3, 4 glucose are known as **epimers**.
37. The most important epimers of glucose are **mannose** and **galactose**.
38. Sugar + keto group = **ketose**.
39. Sugar + aldehyde group = **aldose**.
40. Glycosides are componds formed by the condensation of reaction between **sugar** and hydroxyl group of a second compound **glycine**.
41. Amino sugars (Hexoamines) ex: D-Glucosamine, D-Galactosamine and D-Mannosamine.
42. Glucosamine is a constituent of **hyaluronic acid**.
43. Chitin is a polymer of **N-acetyl glucosamine**.
44. Galactosamineis a constituent of **glycoprotein** and mannosamine is part of **mucoprotein**.
45. Disaccharides – Maltose, Sucrose and Lactose.

46. **Sucrose** is a non-reducing sugar and most abundantly distributed sugar.
47. Fructose is strongly **levorotatory**.
48. Hydrolysis of sucrose yields a crude mixture called **inert sugar**.
49. Honey contains a large proportion of invert sugar.
50. Raffinose is also called **melitose** is a **trisaccaride**.
51. Hot springs in yellow national park provided the first archaeon ***(Thermusaquaticus).***
52. Opportunistic pathogen – ***Pseudomonas aeruginosa.***
53. Plaice – ***Peuronectesplastessa.***
54. Zone of maximum crystallization -1°C to -5°C.
55. Best RSW: CSW ratio is 1:2.

21

Fish Products and Value Addition

1. Protein solubility depends up on the **amino acids composition**
2. Viscosity is influenced by **protein solubility & swelling capacity**
3. Thermodynamically unstable mixture of immiscible liquid are called as **emulsion**
4. Emulsion capacity based on the **hydro pobisity charecters** of myosin
5. Foam is the **analogous** to the **emulsion**
6. **Protein solubility** is the key requisite for foam formation
7. **My of ibrilar** are the largest water holding filament
8. Cross linking of protein polymer called **Gelation**
9. Important key characteristics for gel forming ability is **freshness of the fish**
10. Margarine produces the **golden yellow colour**
11. Lards produce a **pale yellow colour**
12. Plasticity of the fat depends on the **triglycerides** content
13. BHA, BHT & ethoxyquin are **antioxidants**
14. The permitted level of BHA , BHT in the fat are **200mg/ kg** of fat
15. **Sodium nitrite** & **sodium nitrate** are used as a preservatives to prevent the growth of ***C. botulinum***
16. **Sulphites** & **sulphates** are commonly used as a **preservatives**
17. **Sulphite** & **benzoic acids** are the **bacteriosides**
18. **Phospodites (lectines)** are commonly used as a **emulsifier**
19. **Alginic acids, acacia, carageneen** are commonly used as a **stabilizer**
20. **Bixin** and **curcumin** are natural **foodcolour**
21. To inactivate the copper & iron **sequestrants** are used
22. EDTA is a most effective **sequestrants**
23. Sequestrants are used to prevent the **struvite formation**
24. **Humectant** are used to keep bread & cake in most

25. **Anticaking** agent immobilize the water
26. Commonly used humectants are **glycerol**
27. **Eropane 1,2 diol & sorbitol** also used as a humectants
28. Enzyme **papain** are used to **tenderize** the meat
29. To prvent the millard reaction **glucose oxidase** are used
30. Vitamin E is the natural **anti- oxidant**
31. Riboflavin a bright yellow pigment act as a **coenzyme**
32. **Fucellaran** is a thickening agent
33. Yield of deboned meat varies from **35-50%**
34. Ground fish meat paste are **surimi**
35. **Alasca Pollack** (theragrachaleograma) is best suitable for **surimi** production
36. In trophical countries **threadfin bream & scianid** are good sources for **surimi production**
37. In India **lizard fish & threadfin** bream are commonly used for **surimi production**
38. For minced meat washing the ratio of fish meat and water is **1;3**
39. During washing water soluble compounds are washed out,that is called as **leaching**
40. After dewatering the minced meat are called as a crude **surimi**
41. Removing of bones, skins from the minced meat is called as are **refining**
42. Surimi kept in the water both at 40 degree to gel formation that process called as setting or **suwari**
43. Sodiumtripoly phosphate &tetrasodium pyrophosphate are commonly used as a **synergist**
44. The rate of chemical reaction will be **low during** the high concentration of sugars
45. Sarcoplasmic proteins are water **soluble present** in the **cell plasma**
46. **Kamaboko** is the popular sea food in **japan**
47. Steamed kamaboko called as **itasuki**
48. **Broiled** kamaboko are called as **chikuwa** it is **tubular** shape kamaboko
49. Boiled kamaboko are called as **hampen**
50. Fried kamaboko are called as **tempura** .it is also known as **satsumage**
51. Ball and square shaped kamaboko are called as **age kamaboko**

52. Lead shaped – **sasakamaboko**
53. Noodle shaped – **soba kamaboko**
54. Rolled kamaboko – **datemaki**
55. Chipped kamaboko - **kezurikamaboko**
56. A high value functional protein powder was developed by **venugopaletal**
57. Hurdle technology was defined by **listener** in 2000
58. Nisin and natamycin are **antimicrobial agent**
59. Sushi is a **fermented product**
60. Hurdle technology also called as **combined process**
61. **EU** defined **minimally processed** food contain water activity **above 0.85** & PH above **4.5**
62. Codex Alimentarious Commission proposed minimally processed food contain water activity above **0.92 & pH above 4.6**
63. **BADDER** machine are used for **filleting & skinning**
64. Temperature in extruder cooking zone is **80 - 150 deg**
65. The barrel temperature in forming zone is **65 - 95 deg**
66. Extrution moister content range from **25 - 35%**
67. A coated food product also known as **enrobed product**
68. The first commercially successful coated product is **fish finger or fish sticks**
69. Fish **nuggets** are developed from **croaker**
70. **Fish protein hydrolasate** is a by product is prepared from **fish muscle waste**
71. For enzyme hydrolysis **papin & bromoline** are used
72. PHD –partialyhydrolised fish meat is a form of **fish protein concentrate**
73. Fish sausage are prepared from **surimi** are **fish fillet**
74. The texture of the sausage is depend on the **grade of the surimi**
75. **AF2** is a sausage preservatives .but it is **banned in 1974**
76. **Polyvinylidine chloride** are used for packing of sausage
77. Algin gel form with out **heating or cooling**
78. Alginic acids are derived from **brown seaweed**
79. AGAR AGAR derived from **red algae**
80. Commonly occurring agarophites in india are **gracilaria sp, gelidiella**

81. **Philippines** is the world largest producer for carrageenan
82. Important species used for carrageenan preparation is ***chondruscrispis*** (irish mass)
83. **Pure carrageenen** will **not** solidify even its cooled **under freezing point**
84. **Carrageenan** are used as a **stabilizer** for chocolate milk
85. **Carrageenan** is the third most important hydrocolloid
86. **Polyvinylidine chloride** is ideal packaging for **frozen fish curry**
87. Fresh water fishes like **tilapia & catfish** are **suitable** for the production of **coated product**
88. Fish burger also known as **fish patties**. it is similar to the fish cutlet
89. Low pressure extrusion process are widely used for **fish minces**
90. Minced meat technology is most popular in **Japan**
91. **Poly phosphate** are used to prevent the **drip loss**
92. The **USA** is the leading producer for **surimi** followed by japan
93. Sous vide technology also known as **"cusianenpapillote sous vide"**
94. Shark meat contain high amount of **urea**
95. Deep sea shark liver is the richest source of the **squalene**
96. The occurrence of squalene was reported by **Tsujimoto** in **1906**
97. Basking shark contain very high quantity of **squalene**
98. **Glycogen** is a major type carbohydrate present in **fish muscle**
99. Fish have lower glycogen content because fish meat **spoiled quickly**
100. In salmon fat content range from **0.35 - 14%**
101. Ordinary halibut have **glossy meat**
102. The flesh of female species contain more amount of **protein** then the male
103. Sarcoplasmic protein soluble in low **ionic strength solution** (0.15M)
104. Myofibrillar protein soluble **high ionic strength solution** (above 0.5M)
105. Type A - FPC contain **80% of protein** & 0.75% of fat
106. Type B FPC contain **71% of protein & 3% fat**
107. **Azeotropic** extraction used to remove **odoriferous compound**
108. Textured FPC called as **marine beef**
109. **Fixing** is the most important procedure in the manufacturing of insulin

110. **Bagoong** is a fish are or shrimp **paste** obtained by fermentation
111. **Belachan** – fermented shrimp paste
112. Fermented shrimp paste in Thailand known as **KAPPI**, in Burma – NAGAPI, In Indonesia –TRASSI
113. MAM is a **nitrogenous rich** fish paste.it has carbohydrate higher level **(7 - 20%)**
114. **Jeotkal** is a fermented seafood.

22

Fish By-Products and Waste Utilization

1. Fish flesh contains **15 - 20 % protein**.
2. Fish meal is a good source of **Vitamin B**.
3. Fish meal is also a good source of some trace elements which is referred as **unknown growth factors**.
4. **Wet rendering & dry rendering** are the methods of preparing fish meal.
5. Moisture level of the wet rendered fish is **about 8 - 10%**.
6. Stick water = 5.6% of fish solids + 94% of water + 0.4% of oil.
7. Albumin is also present in **stick water**.
8. In direct driers = outlet temperature is maintained as **80 - 100 °C** & inlet temperature is maintained as high as **600 - 800 °C**.
9. Dryers typically designed to dry the wet meal to around **9 - 10%** of moisture content.
10. **Plastics** are chosen for packaging for its oxygen impermeability.
11. **Fish protein concentrate** is a stable fish protein prepared from whole fish or other aquatic animals.
12. **CFPP** – Concentrated Fish Protein Products.
13. The final confirmation of the components of the mixture is about less than **0.1% of lipids**.
14. FPC is prepared from **Viobin** process, **Canadian** process and **Azeo-trophic** mixture.
15. In Viobin process, **ethylene chloride** forms a constant boiling mixture with water boiling at 71°C.
16. In Canadian process employs **Isopropyl alcohol** as the solvent for extraction of lipids.
17. In Azeotrophic mixture extraction method, it involves fish cooking in 0.5% acetic acid for 30 min along with mixture of hexane and ethyl alcohol containing 32.2 moles% of alcohol boiling at 58.68 °C.

18. Textured fish protein concentrate is also called as **Marine Beef**.
19. **Fish liver oils** were used for the **therapeutic purposes** in the treatment of Vitamin A & D deficiencies.
20. The most important sources of the liver oils are **Cod, Haddock and Shark**.
21. Fish oil is prepared from **alkali digestion/ enzyme digestion** method.
22. Vitamin oil is treated with **alkali for digestion** because it secures 70-95% of Vitamin A.
23. Squalene – **shark liver oil**.
24. Squalene is an **unsaturated hydrocarbon** present in the unsaponifiable fraction of fish oils.
25. **Squalene** is used as **bactericide**.
26. **Gelatin** is a protein that **lacks** in an essential amino acid **tryptophan**.
27. **Gelatin** is a protein that has high source of an essential amino acid called as **lysine** and **methionine**.
28. **Gelatin** can be extracted from the **skin and bones of fish**.
29. Gelatin is used for food industry (gelling, stabilizing, emulsifying, dispersing or thickening) ,Industry (photo engraving & chemical itching of metal parts) and optical industry (in formulation of light sensitive material like blue print papers).
30. Fish **glue** can be made from fish **skin and head**.
31. For hydrolysis of the stock into glue, acetic acid is added to act as a catalytic agent.
32. Fish maws are prepared from **swim bladder**.
33. Fish maws are rich in **collagen**.
34. Cleaned and air dried air bladder of fish is called as **fish maw**.
35. Isinglass – **used** as a sizing agent in textiles and as an ingredient in **Indian ink**.
36. Pearl essence is a suspension of **crystalline guanine** in water or an organic solvent.
37. Guanine chemically called as **2 - amino - 6 - oxypyrine**.
38. Fish insulin is fixed by saturated **picric acid**.
39. **Scott** and **Dudley** are the two methods employed in the **insulin extraction**.
40. In Dudley's method, the picrate of insulin is dissolved by **acetone**.

41. In Scott's method, the crushed pancreas extracted by **acidic alcohol with hydrochloric acid**.
42. Technical grade, food and pharmaceutical grade are the two types of grade available for fish **albumin**.
43. Fermented fishery products (popular in South east Asian countries)
    a. Nuoc-mam, nam-pla of Thailand
    b. Nuoc-mam-gau-ca of Khmer Republic
    c. Patis of Philippines
44. Fish **bangoong** is a saline product obtained by partial **fermentation of fish**.
45. Bagoognaalamang is a product obtained by fermenting species of small shrimps mixed with salt.
46. Malaysian **Belachan – shrimp paste** (*Anchoviellacmmersoni* and *A.indica*).
47. Vietnams Mam is differentiated from the fish paste and nuoc-mam by its **higher content of carbohydrates (7-20%)**.
48. **Chao-mam** is called as **sugar syrup**.
49. Indonesian **Trassi** is a paste made from shrimps or small sized fishes.
50. Trassiudang is made from type of plankton consisting of very small shrimps called **rebon**.
51. Korean **jeotkal** – traditional salted and **fermented products** of Korea.
52. Fish silage is **liquefied** fish protein.
53. Fish protein hydrolysate is a **spray dried** product.
54. Shark skin leather is a byproduct of shark fishery where shark liver is still used as a source of **Vitamin A**.
55. **Shark fin rays** are one the most **expensive** fish products in the world.
56. Shark fins over 4-5 feet in length are used for processing.
57. The moisture content of the shark fin after drying is **about 10 – 15%**.
58. Trade expects
    a. Pectoral fin – 50%
    b. Dorsal fin – 25%
    c. Caudal fin – 25%
59. Grade of fins:
    a. Extra large – 40 cm and above
    b. Large – 30 to 40 cm

c. Medium – 20 to 30 cm
d. Small – 10 to 20 cm
e. Very small – 4 to 10 cm
f. Mixed or assorted (processed as fish nets)

60. **Blemishes**, defective cut, burns, curling and insects are the common defects observed in dried shark fins.
61. **Blemishes** are caused by **bad handling** and delay in removing the fins.
62. **Dried fins** are packed in **gunny sacks** which is preferred for breathe.
63. Processed fins may be further processed into **fin needles**.
64. **Fish calcium powder** can be prepared from **backbone of tuna calcium**.
65. Shark cartilage – presence of chondriotinsulphate which is a **mucopolysaccharide**.
66. Processed sea cucumber is also called as **Bech-De-Mer**.
67. Teat fishes (sea cucumbers) are graded based on their **color** (Black/ White).
68. **Cellulose** is the most abundant organic compound on the earth crust.
69. **Chitin** is the **second most** abundant **organic compound** on the earth crust.
70. Deacetylated product of chitin is called as **Chitosan**.
71. Nori / Laver – prepared from ***Porphyralaciniata***.
72. Dried laminaria (Brown algae) seaweed is called as **KOMBHU** in Japan.
73. Dried Undaria – **WAKAME**.
74. **Furcellaran** is extracted primarily from red sea weed *Furcellaria-fastigiata.*
75. Furcellaran gel is strongest gel than agar gel.
76. Furcellaran's chemical structure is similar to kappacarrageenan except it has fewer sulfate groups in the molecule.
77. Porphyran – sulfated polysaccharide.
78. Porphyran is an another phycocolloid derived from *porphyra* spp.,
79. **Funorin** – Solubilized **sea weed product**.
80. Funorin found in ***Gloiopeltis* sp**.

23

Microbiology of Fish and Fishery Products

1. **Bacteria intoxication** – already formed bacteria not live bacteria
2. Bacterial infection - **consumption of live bacteria**
3. Neuro toxin produced by ***C. botulinum***
4. Listeria identified by the **serotyping**
5. Fishery product have type E, ***C. botulinum***
6. *S. aureus* produced entiro toxin
7. **S. aureus** is heat resistant but not active in pasteurization
8. E. coli – **0157: H7**
9. Salmonella should be below **105/ g**
10. Septicemia can occur due to the **salmonella**
11. L. monocytogens should be **10/ g**
12. **V. parahaemolyticus** is the autochthonous marine bacteria
13. The permitted level of V. parahaemolyticus should be **104/ g**
14. Water activity of most fresh fish about **0.99**
15. Bacterial Spoilage not occurred in the water activity **below the 0.91**
16. Microbes grow well in **0.995 - 0.998**
17. Spoilage of yeast will not occur below the **0.88**a_w
18. Spoilage of mold will not occur below the **0.8** a_w
19. Spoilage of xerophilic mold will not occur below the **0.61**a_w
20. Spoilage of Halophile bacteria will not occur below the **0.75** a_w
21. Bacteria not grown in below **PH of 4**
22. Loss of electron known as **oxidation**
23. Gain of electron known as **reduction**
24. Microbial load in fish skin = **10^2-10^7 cfu/ g**
25. Microbial load in fish gill = **10^3-10^9 cfu/ g**

26. Microbial load in fish intestine = **10^3-10^9 cfu/ g**
27. Crustacean have microbial load about = **10^3 -10^7 cfu/ g**
28. **Kircher** was the first person to observe the decaying bodies
29. **Pastier** was the first person to analyses the role of microbes
30. Enzyme reaction is depends on **the temperature**
31. Activity of microorganism is decreased in **2 fold by reducing** the every **10^0C**
32. Fresh fish from **temperate** water have **longer self-life** then the warm water fishes
33. Food spoilage bacteria have **less resistant** to **freezing**
34. Reducing of **potential spoilage** organism by heating is known as **pasteurization**
35. Heat resistant's but not spore forming bacteria –**mycobacterium tuberculosis**
36. Destruction of all viable microorganism is known as **sterilization**
37. **Bacterial spore** have **more** heat **resistant** then the vegetative cell
38. Long chain fatty acids have **more heat** resistant
39. Sugars will increase the **heat resistant**
40. D- value also known as **decimal reduction value**
41. Times required at specified temperature to kill the 90 % microorganism is known as **D – value**
42. D- value lower in **acidic food**
43. Degree of Fahrenheit required for thermal destruction curve to drop log cycle is known as **Z value**
44. F value also called as **TDT value**
45. 12 D concept mainly used in **low acid canned food**
46. Low moister food do not contain moisture level more than **25 % & a_w of o.6**
47. Killing of micro-organism in food using the electromagnetic radiation without raising temperature as **cold sterilization**
48. Ionizing radiation should be below **2000 A^0**
49. Gama rays penetrate up to **20 cm**
50. REP= absorption of **83 ergs/ g** radiation
51. Radicidation is equal to the **pasteurization**

52. Radio resistant organism ***Deinococcus radiophilus***
53. **GRS-** generally recognized as safe
54. Permitted level of benzoic acid **0.1%**
55. Permitted level of parabens **0.1%**
56. The membrane filter has pore size **0.45 micron**
57. Lactose broth – **E. coli**
58. Bair parker agar used for – **staphylococcus**
59. Bismuth sulphides agar used for – **salmonella**
60. TCBS agar used for – **vibrio**
61. For pour plate sample are added **-1 ml**
62. For spread plate sample are added – **0.1 ml**
63. **ATP measurement** is done by firefly- **luciferein luciferase system**
64. Thermostable nucleus test are used to detect the presence of ***S. aureus***
65. In quick freezing temperature is lowered **-20 ^{0} C within 30 min**
66. In slow freezing temperature is lowered to **-20 ^{0}C within 3- 72 hours**
67. **Tylosin** is the gram positive bacteria **inhibit** the protein synthesis
68. Natamycin is isolated from the ***Streptomyces natalensis***
69. Heat resistant of spore due to **calcium & dipicolinic** acid
70. Most food poisoning is caused by type **A or D *Staphylococcus***

24

Quality Assurance of Fish and Fishery Products

1. Degree of excellence referred as **quality**
2. More acidic pH leads to **chalkiness** in seer fish
3. Low post mortem pH leads to **gapping**
4. In squid and herring **anisakis parasite** normally found
5. The most crustacean parasites are **copepods**
6. **Greasy haddock** is a fungal disease caused by ***icthyosporidium hoferi***
7. Tetra toxin is caused by ***V.alginolyticus***
8. NSP produced by **brevetoxin**
9. VSP- venerupin shellfish poisoning also called as **oyster or asaripoisoning** it is caused by ***Prorocentrum* sp.**
10. Erythematius shellfish poisoning affect the **blood circulatory system**
11. The maximum permitted limit of DDT is **5 mg\ kg**
12. The maximum permitted level of deldrin is **0.30 mg\ kg**
13. In fish mineral oil contamination leads to **tainted odour**
14. During oxidation red pigment change in **yellow colour**
15. The substances responsible for odour of the fish is **DMS**
16. Odour of fish due to consumption of **pteropod**. It contain **dimethyl-b-propothtin**
17. Earthy odour of fish is caused by **geosmin**
18. Muddy odour is caused by microalgae **actinomycetes**
19. If fish is more affected by microbes it is called **stinker or bilgy fish**
20. **Hypoxanthin** have bitter taste
21. Mortality due to infection of listeria monocytogenes are **29%**
22. ***L.monocytogens*** is an facultative intra cellular pathogen
23. ***listeria*** are heat resistant bacteria

24. *listeria* identified by **serotyping** it have 7 type.
25. Thermal death time of listeria monocytogenes are **D60 being 4.5 min**
26. *Clostridium botulinum* classified in to **7 type**
27. ***Clostridium botulinum*** type E is most important
28. In clostridium botulinum type A,B,F is **proteolytic**
29. In clostridium botulinum type E is **non protiolytic**
30. *C.botulinum* majority of outbreak occurred in **fermented fish**
31. **E.coli** and **salmonella** can grow in **esturine water**
32. ***Salmonella*** can survive in **drying** and thus be problem in **fish meal**
33. Smoked fish is a traditional sources of **salmonellosis**
34. *V. colerae* is **facultative anerobic**
35. *V.colerae* **halophilic** in nature
36. *V. colerae* having **gun shot motility** or darting moyility
37. *V.colera* produce **entero toxin**
38. *V.parahaemoliticus* was first isolated in **japan** in 1950
39. The permitted level of PSP is **80 microgram\ 100 G**
40. The permitted level of DSP **20 mg\ 100g**
41. The permitted level of NSP is **20 mouse unit**
42. Permitted limt of ASP is **20 mg\ kg**
43. To reduce the blackening **sodium or metabisulphite** are used in dip 1-2 min
44. To prevent the weight loss **phosphate** are used
45. The water vapourtransmition rate in frozen storage fish should be **50g\ m seq\ day**
46. The permitted level of **E.coli** in fish is **20\ g**
47. *S.aureus* should not be more than **100\ g**
48. In frozen **sword fish & tuna greendiscoloration** is more important
49. The sturvite formation will be occur in the **thunnusalalunga**
50. To prevent the sturvite formation **0.5% sodium hexameta phosphate** are used
51. High **TMAO** content found in the **tail end of the tuna**
52. TMAO is responsible for **greening in tuna**
53. Flat sour spoilage Is due to **bacillus sterothermophilus**

54. Bluing can be prevented by proper bleeding at the time of **butchering** (or) by adding EDTA salt
55. The canned shrimp should have a moisture content **72%**
56. **Poly cyclic aromatic carbon** involved in smoking
57. **Phenolic** compound are most effective in **preserving of fish**
58. **Bensopyrine** and **poly aromatic corbon** are highly carcinogenic
59. **Formaldehyde** is an antifungal agent
60. **Phenol** have **anti-microbial** and **anti-oxidant** effect
61. The spoiled fish smoking will leads to **colour change**
62. Packing warm smoked product closely can leads to **sweating**
63. **Browning & tanning** is the quality defect in the **smoked fish**
64. Formation of secondary skin is known as **tanning**
65. The tanning is based on reaction of **carbonyl & protein**
66. **Xerophilic mould** involve in formation of spoilage in **smoked fish**
67. **Ropy brine** will occur during pickling of whole herring using **mixture of salt & sucrose**
68. Salt fish have 4 types of microbial deterioration they are **slime, putty, pink & dun**
69. The deterioration **putty occurs** in the **thick parts** of the fish
70. When salt concentration high **halophiles** will cause the **pink spoilage**
71. Dun spoilage are caused by **halophilic fungi**
72. The halophilic fungi are **wallemia or oospora**
73. **Pink and dun** spoilage are occurred due to **high salt content**
74. Pink & dun spoilage can be prevented by adding **3% sodiumpropinate & 97% sodium chloride**
75. **Rust** spoilage is due to oxidation of fat in the atmospheric oxygen
76. **Maggot** infestation caused in **salted fish**
77. Perrmited level of pyrethrins is **3mg\ kg**
78. **ICMF** – International Commission on Microbiological specification of Food
79. TBT – Technical Barrier of Trade in **1995**
80. HACCP – was initially developed by **Pillsbury company**
81. The best method of retaining natural quality in **dried squid is freeze drying**

82. To avoid case hardening **cooking** before **drying** is done
83. The storage place of dried product should not have relative **humidity above 75%**
84. To control the insect infection **methyl bromide** is used to **fumigation** of dry fish storage space
85. **Lipid peroxide** is an intermediate product of **oxidation**
86. Lipid peroxide can be destroy the **vit A& E**
87. Moist fish is susceptible to damage **blow files** and their larvae
88. Fatty fishes & **herring** make the best **traditional marinades**
89. **Hexmethyline tetramine** is a bacteriocides
90. Cooking of fish in **pre –or in rigor** may present **quality problem**
91. In fish sausage slime formation is due to ***Streptococcus, Leuconostoc, Micrococcus***
92. Softening of sausage is due to ***Bacillus***
93. In sausage block spot is due to ***B.coagulants, Lactobacillus sp***.
94. *Bacillus* is the prime spoiler in the **surimi**
95. Sensory or organo-leptic evaluation is fully depends on the **human sense**
96. Torrymeter has reading **from 0-16**
97. **"bionic" nose** is used to test the **odour of the fish** .it is developed by university of Nagasaki
98. Protein content is accessed by determining the nitrogen content of the sample and multiplying it by a **factor 6.25**
99. Nitrogen is commonly determined by the **Kjeldhal** method and **biuret method**
100. Fat can be determined by the **Soxhelt Apparatus** and **Blige & Dyer extraction**
101. The spoilage bacteria produce **H_2S, TMA & Ammonia**
102. Volatile sulphur compounds are produced by ***Pseudomonas***
103. The formaldehyde fixes the **ammonia & DMA**
104. Fish flesh start visible spoilage bacteria level **10^7 oganisms\ g**
105. To measure the TMA content **dyers pirate has been used**
106. TMA is more sensitive **indicator of spoilage**

107. Hypoxanthin can be measured by **enzyme method** using the **xanthium oxidase**
108. K value expresses the relationship between **inosine, hypoxanthin & the total amount of ATP related compound**
109. K value of fresh fish various from **20 - 25%**
110. The spoilage fish contain **K value 50 - 60%**
111. In sword fish formation of **hypoxanthinis low** so that it concentration is useless as index of spoilage
112. Maximum permissible level of hypoxanthin content in fish should be **2.5 micro moles\ g**
113. The enzyme used for distinguish the fresh fish &frozen fish is **malic enzyme**
114. Fresh& frozen fish can be distinguished by measuring the activity of enzymes like **nutralbetta – N acetylglucosaminidase**
115. When the **TPC reaches 10^7 \ g** the fish is found to be spoiled
116. The intrinsic bacterial flora on fish is predominantly **psychrophilic**
117. The indicator of fecal pollution is **E.coli & fecal streptococci**
118. Indicator of personal hygiene is ***Staphylococcus***
119. *Feacal streptococci* count in frozen shrimp should be **100cfu\ g**
120. The maximum allowable limit of *S.aureus* is **100cfu\ g**
121. A selective media more widely used for the isolation and enumeration of **staphylococcus** is **potassium tellurite of BPA** (baird parker agar)
122. For dye reduction test **resazurin & methelene blue** are the most commonly used dye
123. To **measure** the endotoxins. the best method known as **limulus amoebocyte lysate**
124. Limulus amoebocyte lysate is obtained from **horseshoe crab**
125. In electric impedance test .impedance change are detected when the concentration of micro organism the level of **10^6 -10^7 cells\ ml**
126. The lowest level of sampling in the codex sampling plans **n = 6, c = 1**.
127. **SSOP** - sanitation standered operating procedure
128. **SCP** - sanitation control procedure
129. Water used in the processing plant the level of **available chlorine 5-10 ppm**

130. In ice manufacturing water should contain the level **available chlorine is 5 - 10 ppm**
131. ISI started in **1947**
132. Export act - **1963**
133. The inspection scheme for FFP (fish &fishery product) was taken over by EIA effect from **1st may 1969**
134. ISO – international organization for standardization was established in **1946 at Geneva** (Switzerland)
135. **ISO 9000 standards** have 17 elements
136. Codex Alimentarius commission jointly brought out by the **FAO & WHO**
137. EU has specified **62 parameters**

25

Fish Curing

1. In India roughly curing preserves 20% of the fish caught.
2. **Salt curing** is an important and one of the most widely adopted method of fish preservation.
3. **Higher salt content** prevents the growth of normal spoilage micro flora in the fish.
4. Salted fish reduced to biscuit cure in **drying kilns**.
5. Sodium chloride diffuses through the fish flesh by a dialysis mechanism & water will diffuse to the outside due to the osmotic pressure between the brine and fish muscle solution.
6. **Gaspe** curing is practiced in **aboard**, originated in **eastern Canada**.
7. Dry salting ratio is **1:3 to 1:10** (salt: fish).
8. Yield of dry salting is about **35-40%**
9. The shelf life of the dry salted fish is about **6-10 weeks**.
10. The moisture content of the wet salted fish is about **50-55%**.
11. Wet salted fishes are more suspected to **fungal growth, bacterial degradation** and general putrefaction.
12. **Mono curing** is done on medium to small sized fishes.
13. The yield of the mono cured fish is about **70%**.
14. The shelf life of the mono cured fishes is about **50 days**.
15. The fish is mixed with salt in the ratio of **4:1 for pit curing**.
16. Pit cured fishes were normally called as **KUZHI KARUVADU**.
17. The shelf life of pit cured fishes is about **20 days**.
18. **Colombo curing** was practiced by the fishermen of South Canara and Malabar regions of the **West coast of India**.
19. Mackerel, Sardine and Non-fatty pelagic fishes are **suitable for Colombo curing**.
20. **Gorukapuli** – *Garciniacambogia.*

21. There are four types of salt found – solar, brine-evaporated, rock and manufactured salt.
22. Rock salt – **80 to 99% of NaCl**.
23. Purified manufactured salt contain – **99.9% of NaCl**.
24. The impurities of common salt **Calcium and Magnesium chlorides** slow down the penetration of salt into the fish, thus increasing the spoilage rate.
25. **Tracescopper** appearance to the fish making it **look spoiled**.
26. Excessive quantities of calcium and magnesium compounds impart **taste** to fish and make it **brittle** when dry.
27. Halophilic moulds – **Dun spoilage**.
28. Tropical ambient temperature, the decomposition to centre of thick muscles before the salt concentration had reached levels high enough to prevent bacterial spoilage is called as **putty fish** and is also often associated with Ca^{2+} and Mg^{2+} ions of impure salts binding with protein and forming a barrier to the passage of Na^{2+} ions to the thicker part of the flesh.
29. Lipolysis and oxidative rancidity play an important role in the flavor of low fat, cured white fish products.
30. ***Pseudomonas* spp. are halophobic** and will **not grow** in salt concentrations exceeding **5%**.
31. *Staphylococcus aureus* is a **halotolerant** (10 - 20%) grow in salt environment.
32. Drying under controlled conditions is called as **dehydration**.
33. The microbiological growth is completely arrested below a water activity of **0.6 a_w**.
34. Lipid oxidation at very low water activity.
35. **Psychrometrics** – wet and dry bulb hygrometer.
36. Sun drying is also called as **natural drying**.
37. RH above **70 - 75%** will not help to dry the fish to the desired level.
38. Solar tent drier, air temperature is known to rise to the levels of **60 °C**.
39. The most hygienic method for sun drying them on racks is called as **rack drying**.
40. Cold smoking - **35 °C**.
41. Hot smoking – **60 - 80 °C**.

42. Electric smoking – **corona discharge**.
43. Electric smoking was invented by **Toriyama**.
44. In liquid smoking, the liquids are prepared by dry **distillation of wood**.
45. **Masmin** is a traditional smoke cured product of Lakshadweep Islands and Maldives.
46. **Katsuo-bushi** – dried bonito sticks.
47. Jelly fish belngs to class **Scyphozoa**.
48. Dehydrated jelly fish is not strictly dried product which has **55 - 60%** of moisture content.
49. Jelly fish – white type – widely distributed in the East and Southeast region of China.
50. Marinades are fish or shellfish preserved in a mixture of **acetic acid and salt**.

Fisheries Engineering and Post Harvest Management

26

Aquaculture Engineering

1. **Farm** is complex structure comprising **living and non-living** things.
2. The engineering components and structures – basic necessities of an aqua farm.
3. **Ponds, Water transportation** systems – primary structures of an aqua farm.
4. Machineries, builtin structures and other peripheral accessories – secondary structuresof an aqua farm.
5. Secondary structures may vary from one pond to another pond based on the
   a. Type of culture
   b. Method followed
   c. Economic status of the farmer.
6. **Site selection – Pre-requisites** of a successful aquaculture farm.
7. Soil bottom must be impervious to **prevent excessive seepage**.
8. Fine textured soils – a **high clay** content.
9. Embankment ponds are also called as **Hill/ Water shed ponds**.
10. **Excavated ponds** are principally used for the commercial fish and shrimp production.
11. Layout of the farm depends on **topography and shape** of the area.
12. Pond orientation should be parallel to the direction of the **prevailing wind**.
13. Extensive farm = **5 ha**.
14. Semi intensive farm = **0.25-1 ha**.
15. Intensive farm = **0.025 – less than 0.25 ha**.
16. Principal qualities of dikes – **Solidity and water tightness**.
17. **Sandy clay** – best material for the construction of the dike.

18. Inside slope ratio of the pond
    a. **1:2** for clayey soil
    b. 1:3 for sandy or silty soil
19. Outside slope ratio of the pond is **1:1.5**.
20. The space between dike surface and surface of the pond water is called **free board** of the pond.
21. **Turfing** – plantation of grass over the dikes to prevent erosion by the waves.
22. **Sluice** – two lateral and parallel walls.
23. **Monk** - two lateral and parallel walls with a **back wall**.
24. **Sluice** may be constructed as **both** at an inlet and outlet.
25. Monk **never** used at the **inlet**.
26. The earthen enclosures covering all the sides of the pond to retain water inside are called as **bundhs**.
27. Sides of the bundh are called as **slopes**.
28. The flat portion at the bottom of the slope just above the pond bottom is called as **bench** or **berm**.
29. RCC –Reinforced Cement Concrete ponds.
30. Area of nursery ponds – **0.005 to 0.05 ha**.
31. Volume of earth in m^3= [(a*b) + (b*d)]*l (if slopes are identical)
32. Volume of earth in m^3= [(a*b) + (b*d)/ 2 + (b*e)/2]*l (if slopes are un-identical).
33. Area occupied by the bundh base
    a. For identical slopes (2d + a)*l.
    b. For un-identical slopes (a+d+e)*l.
34. Quantum of water that is flowing through a channel is the product of **cross sectional area** of the channel and the **flow velocity**.
    a. Q =A*V
35. Factor expressing the degree of roughness is called as **Roughness co-efficient**.

27

Refrigeration and Equipment Engineering

1. The process of removing heat from a substances under controlled condition known as **refrigeration**.
2. A refrigerator is a **revised heat engine**.
3. Whenever a force acts on body and the body undergoes a displacement is known as **work**.
4. The rate of doing work – **power**.
5. Unit of work - **kgf, Nm, joule**.
6. 1 HP-**736 watts**.
7. Energy defined as the **capacity to do work**.
8. 1 bar- **105N/ m^2**.
9. **Absolute pressure** = gauge pressure + atmosphere pressure.
10. The degree of hotness or coolness is known as **temperature**.
11. The level of **intensity** of the body – heat.
12. The absolute temperature scale having only **positive values**.
13. Freezing point of solid CO_2 is **-78 ^{0}C**.
14. Freezing point of O_2 is **-183 ^{0} C**.
15. Conversion formula = **C/ 100 = F- 32/ 180**.
16. **CHU** - centrifuge heat unit.
17. **BTU** - British thermal unit.
18. The amount heat required to raise the temperature of one pound water through 1 ^{0} F is known as **BTU**.
19. The heat which causes a change in temperature in a substances at constant rate is known as **sensible heat**.
20. The latent heat also known as **hidden heat**.
21. The amount heat added or removed to produce only the phase change at constant temperature is known as – **latent heat**.

22. The latent heat of melting of ice is **80 Kcal/ kg**.
23. Absolute humidity is the **mass of water divided by a unit of air.**
24. **Relative humidity** = amount of water vapor present in the air/ maximum amount that the air could contain at the temperature.
25. A slower method of heat transfer is **convection**.
26. **Enthalpy** is defined as the total heat energy contained a gas.
27. In **adiabatic system** there is no heat transfer in to or out of the system.
28. Isentric process in which **entropy** of the fluid remain constant.
29. Isochoric process – constant **volume** process.
30. Isobaric process – constant **pressure** process.
31. **Throttling process** - no change in enthalpy.
32. First law of thermodynamics - **law of conservation of energy**.
33. The second law of thermodynamics - **law of degradation of energy**.
34. Entropy – **measure of unusable energy**.
35. C. botulinum required **4.5 M rad** of radiation.
36. Half-life of cobalt - **5.3 year**.
37. Ammonia - **R 717**.
38. Boiling point of ammonia **(-33°C)**.
39. Carbon dioxide - **R 744**.
40. Sulphur dioxide – **R764**.
41. The boiling point of SO_2 – **(-10°C)**.
42. Methyl chloride – **R40**.
43. Boiling point of methyl chloride **(-23.7°C)**.
44. Air – **R729**.
45. Freon -11 **(CCL_3F)**.
46. R- 11 are widely used in **air conditioning** the colour of cylinder R-11 used is **orange**.
47. Boiling point of R-11 is **-23°C**.
48. The cylinder colour for R-12 is **white**.
49. R-21 are widely used in **house hold refrigerator.**
50. R-21 has boiling point about **48 °F**.
51. The cylinder code for R-22 is **green**.
52. Corrosion inhibitor – **sodium dichromate**.

53. To correct the excessive alkalinity **dichromate** are used.
54. Water - **R718**.
55. The improved type of air refrigeration cycle is **vapor compression cycle**.
56. In vapor absorption system instead of compressor generator **absorbent assembly** are used.
57. Expansion valve also called as **throttle valve or melting device**.
58. In vapor absorption system **R20 ,R12, and ammonia** are used.
59. The compressor is a **heart** of a refrigeration system.
60. The centrifugal compressor for refrigeration system was designed by **Dr. Willis and H. carrier**.
61. The head constitutes **10 - 20% body weight**.
62. The de boner machine are usually **3 -7 mm** in diameter.
63. **Cellulose** is a ecofriendly cheap material.
64. **Fiber glass** is a most common type of insulation.
65. The recommended storage temperature for all fishery products is **-18°C**
66. The insulation materials. The thermal conductance should not exceed **0.15 Kcal /m^2 h °C**.
67. The fins are made up of **aluminum**.
68. **Suction pressure** – absolute pressure of refrigerant at the **inlet** of compressors.
69. **Discharge pressure** – it is the absolute pressure of refrigerant at the **out let** of compressor.
70. **Compression ratio** – ratio of total cylinder volume to the clearance volume.
71. The liquid nitrogen freezer do not require **compressor, condenser**.
72. Lquid nitrogen **freezer 4 times** more costlier then the air blast freezer.
73. Carbon dioxide freezer would not be suitable for **remote sensing area**.
74. **Copper tubes** are not used in ammonia refrigerating system.

28

Fishing Craft Technology

1. The removal of moister from the timber is known as **seasoning**.
2. For boat building purpose timber should have moisture about **18-20%**.
3. Mild steel contain **0.15 - 0.30%** of carbon.
4. Low carbon steel contain **less than 0.15%** of carbon.
5. High carbon steel contain **0.8- 1.5%** of carbon.
6. The specific gravity of steel **7.84**.
7. The aluminum boat was firstly built in France **1892**.
8. Ferro cement boat was introduced in France – **1847**.
9. Specific gravity of aluminum – **2.7**.
10. Specific gravity of Ferro cement **2.4 - 2.6**.
11. GRP boat was first introduced by USA at 1946.
12. In india FRP was introduced in **1968**.
13. Forward end of hull is **bow**.
14. The top portion of the hull is known as **deck**.
15. The shell of the hull is known as **plating**.
16. The upper most rows of side plating are called **sheer strakes.**
17. The speed length known as **Fraud's number**.
18. The measurement of ship capacity – **tonnage**.
19. **Dredges** are used to collect the mollusk from the bottom.
20. Machwa, Bedi – **Gujarat**.
21. Dhonies – **Rameshwaram**.
22. The traditional fishing craft of Goa are **dugout canoe**.
23. **Rampani** boats are popular in northern Karnataka.
24. In **southern** Karnataka – dugout canoe.
25. Sound wave travels in the water at rate of **1500m/ sec**.

26. The difference between the fish and bottom can be differentiated by the **white line technic.**
27. **Caulking** – making water boat tight.
28. **Copper sheathing** is the most ideal for protection of underwater part of the hull.
29. IMCO - comes in to existence in **1959**.
30. In India regulation for the fishing gear is governed by **Merchant shipping act** (44) - 1958.
31. Harbour craft rules formed under the Indian port act (XV) - **1908**.
32. The distance GZ known **as righting arm**.
33. For stable equilibrium **B must same vertical line G** and **G must be below** M.
34. Nutral equilibrium **when M and G are coincident**.
35. For trawler minimum GZ should be 40 cm.
36. For purse seiner minimum GZ should be 45 cm.
37. **BHP - it is the power available at the cranck shaft of the engine to perform work. BHP = IHP - frictional losses in gear**
38. **IHP = power produced inside the engine**.
39. **SHP = power required at the end propeller shaft**.
40. **Gallows are used in trawler and purse seiner**.
41. **Davits are used in purse seiner and gill netter**.
42. **Gantry is a 4 in 1 contrivance**.

29

Navigation and Seamanship

1. The process of directing or conducting the movement of vessel one place to another place is known as **navigation**.
2. Controlling the ship is known as **seamanship**.
3. VHF used up to **25 nautical miles**.
4. Speed of sound wave **322m/ sec**.
5. Speed of radio wave **3x10^8 m/ sec**.
6. Navigation derived from **latin** word.
7. Earliest form of navigation is **piloting**.
8. Dead reckoning is **rough** method only.
9. Radio navigation also known as **electronic piloting**.
10. World chart produced by **Gerardus Mercator**.
11. 1^0 will indicate **60 nautical mile**.
12. 1^1 indicate **60 sec**.
13. Department of Indian navy based at **Dehradun**.
14. The axis on which earth rotate is called **geographic polar axis**.
15. 1 nautical mile = **6076.1 feet**.
16. 1 statute mile = **5280 feet (1585m)**.
17. 1 NM = **1.852km**.
18. 1 minute of latitude equal to **1 nautical mile**.
19. Unit of speed commonly used in navigation – **knots**.
20. True direction is expressed in reference to the **geographic pole**. It should be written in **3 digit code**.
21. Rhumb line also known as **loxodromes**.
22. The **magnetic compass** was the only instrument available onboard a vessel for determining the direction.
23. When latitude is above the 75^0 accuracy of **gyrocompass** will decrease
24. Echo-sounder also known as **fathometer**.
25. Echo-sounder has **4 basic** compounds.

26. Pulse power of echo-sounder between **100 - 1000 watts**.
27. Echo-sounder frequency for fisheries **38 KHZ, 120 KHZ, 400 KHZ**.
28. In man over board 4 types of turning are used.
29. In night or reduced visibility – **Williamson turn are used**.
30. When clearly visible – **Anderson turn used**.
31. Separation of desired signals from the other is called **tuning**.
32. Distress calls - **MAYDAY MAYDAY**, channel number 16, 2182 KHZ.
33. Urgency – **PAN PAN**, channel number 16, and 2182 KHZ.
34. Decca is a hyperbolic radio navigation it works at frequency **70-130 KHZ.**
35. Sea-anchor will not touch to the bottom .it is kind of **break for vessel**.
36. Fisherman anchor – **admirality** anchor or kedge type.
37. Stockless anchor is the **most popular anchor**.
38. grapnel anchor is a **light weight anchor**, it is used to quick stop.
39. SONAR originally called as **ASDIC**.
40. SONAR transducer operate **horizontally**.
41. SONAR able to rotates **360^{0}**.
42. LEADLINE is used to measure **depth**. It contain tapered bar of weighing from **7-20** pounds.
43. LEADLINE have **9 marks & 11 deeps**.
44. Deep sea LEADLINE contain **30 - 50 pounds** weight lead.
45. In magnetic compass **32 points** are present each point contain **11.1/ 4°C**
46. The angler difference between true north &magnetic meridian called **variation**.
47. A joining place of equal variation is known as **isogonic line**.
48. Difference between magnetic north and compass north known as **deviation**.
49. The sum of variation and deviation error is called **compass error**.
50. Dry card compass having lightweight Aluminium ring with dia **254 mm**.
51. **Lubber line** represent the direction of the ship head.
52. **Non-magnetic** material are used to construct the **binnacle**.
53. Dry card compass is **sensitive** to rolling and pitching.
54. Wet cardis attached to **nickel–silver** float chamber it is used to **avoid corrosion**.

55. In wet card compass the using liquid are mixture of **distilled water & pure ethyl alcohol**.
56. GPS global positioning system.
57. GPS was launched **1978**.
58. In GPS 24th satellite used in **1994**.
59. At a time we can get **4 satellite** signals in any position of earth.
60. In **Bahamian moor** one anchor off **the bow** and one off the **stern**.
61. **EPIRB** - emergency position indicating radio beacon.
62. **RCC** - rescue coordinating center.
63. EPIRB operate at frequency **121.5MHZ** or 243 MHZ.
64. The EPIRB has **15 ground** station.
65. **Oscar flag** used to express **man over board**.
66. Q- turn also called as **figure eight turn**.
67. RDF often reffered as **radio compass**.
68. To measure the speed of the moving vessel **speed logs** are used.
69. Co_2 extinguishes used for type **B fire**.
70. **Sodium bicarbonate** is the dry chemical extinguishing agent.
71. **Soda acid** fire extinguisher is used to **type A fire**
72. **Foam extingusher** can be used for class A & B fire.
73. Carbon dioxide gas extinguisher can be used in all type fire.
    The colour coding for extinguisher is
    Water- red
    Foam – green
    Dry powder- blue
    Co_2–black
74. Net sonde is also called as **trawl eye**.
75. OMEGA navigation system also **hyperbolic navigation system** developed by **US**.
76. VHF – is transmitted with in the frequency range **156 - 162 MHZ**.
77. VHF also called as **line of sight radio**.
78. Signal T- tango indicate **pair trawling**.
79. Signal Z-zulu indicate **shooting net**.
80. GRT presentation of echo signals is sometimes known as **fish - loop**.
81. In echo sounder depth adjusted automatic amplification is known as **time varied gain**.

30

Fishing Gear Technology

1. **Fiber** are basic material for constructing the gear.
2. Fibers length will be **200 times** greater than that width.
3. Cotton fibber have length about **20 - 50 mm**.
4. Ramie , hemp , liner are also known as **soft fiber**.
5. Ramie fiber – **china grass**.
6. Sisal and manila fiber are **hard fiber**.
7. Poly amide also known as **nylon**.
8. Polystyrene also known as **terylene**.
9. Poly condensation water eliminating process eg **PA, PES**.
10. **Poly vinyl chloride** is the first synthetic fiber to be produced by on an industrial scale. And also first synthetic material for gear.
11. The mixture of vinylidene & vinyl alcohol gives **poly vinylidene chloride**.
12. Continuous filaments are made in **PA, PES, PP**.
13. Staple fiber available in **PA & PES**.
14. Mono filaments are most **PE**.
15. Split fiber are mainly available in **PP**.
16. PP, PE **float** in water.
17. To distinguish the PE & PP **melting test** are used.
18. Density is expressed as grams per cubic meter **(g/ cm^3)**.
19. **PVD** has highest density followed by PES.
20. PVD has density about **1.70**.
21. **Dynamometer** are used to measure the breaking strength.
22. Breaking strength is expressed as the **tensile strength** and **tensity**.
23. Tensile strength is expressed as – **kg/ mm^2**.
24. PA has **high elastic** property.

25. Synthetic material has **less towing** resistance.
26. PES has high **resistance to acid**.
27. PVAA is graded as **resistant**.
28. The basic material for constructing the twisted netting is **single yarn**.
29. Braiding also called **plaiting**.
30. For gill net and seines **soft and medium** twist are used.
31. Hard twist are used in **trawls**.
32. **Extra hard twist** are used in line and rope.
33. Yarn number is expressed as **mass per unit length**.
34. The most commonly used system for denoting the size of yarn is **denier system**.
35. The most commonly used **nylon yarn** for netting Twines is **210 denier**.
36. Denier and Tex system are **direct numbering** system.
37. Metric system has symbol **'Nm'**.
38. British system expressed by **'Ne'**.
39. Combination rope are used in **trawling**.
40. To distinguish the **manila and sisal, burning** test are used.
41. Wood has buoyancy is **650g/ 1000cc**.
42. Cork has buoyancy is **825g/ 1000cc**.
43. **Thermo Cole** has buoyancy about **900/ 1000cc**.
44. Strong plastic has buoyancy about **800-860g/ 1000cc**.
45. Glass float can with stand pressure about **4oo m**.
46. Aluminum has with stand about pressure up to **80 m**.
47. Hydrodynamics float has **v shape bottom**.
48. **Siamese twin** float is made by joining two spherical aluminum floats with curved collar.
49. Inflatable float used in **curved trawler**.
50. Specific gravity of lead - **11.3**.
51. Specific gravity of iron - **7.9**.
52. Specific gravity of clay - **2.2.**
53. **Dahn buoy** is used in set gill net and **Danish seine**.
54. In anchor the terminal part of the shank connecting to the arm called **crown**.

55. The triangular structure in anchor is known as **flukes**.
56. The sharp end of the flukes known as **bills**.
57. The anchor is handled by **gravity band**.
58. Fisherman anchor also called as **admiralty anchor.**
59. Danforth anchor **American design.**
60. CQR is a stock **less anchor**.
61. **Patent stockless anchor**. two arm can move about 45^0 on either side of shank.
62. Patent type anchor mainly used in **large vessel.**
63. Thimble set in **eye of the rope**.
64. Shackle is a **connecting device**.
65. D-shackle are used to **connect the rope**.
66. U- shape shackle known as **straight shackle**.
67. Swivel used to prevent the **twisting**.
68. In troll line swivel used between the **line & snood wire**.
69. The **Norwegian method** of numbering hooks are followed in India.
70. Double hooks are used in **troll**.
71. PES have **high specific gravity.**
72. **PES & PA** continuous filaments are the most favored material for a **pure seine**.
73. **PA** continuous filament preferred for the **gill net**.
74. The percentage of the tannin in the solution should be **4 - 6%**.
75. The readymade tannin extract available in the market is known as **cutch**.
76. Tannin fixation by **$CuSO_4$** Dutch method.
77. The tar is diluted with kerosene or turpentine in the ratio of **3:1**.
78. **Garnol, guprinol** preservatives are used to preserve the net.
79. The initial row of **clove hitch** is known as setting up row.
80. The two sides of the netting along width are called **selvedges.**
81. **Baiting** – reduces the mesh number.
82. **Creasing** – increasing the mesh number.
83. Fly meshing only **two knots** used.
84. Fly meshing reduce the depth of the breath of the netting by **one mesh in one row.**

85. The first clove hitch made is called a **Halfer**
86. In **bar cut** cutting is done in only **one legs in each knot**
87. **Mesh cut** – cutting is done in **two legs** in each knot
88. The length of final rope and its ratio is called as **hanging coefficient**
89. Vertical hanging coefficient – **square root of 1-E^2**
90. Simplest and easiest method of mounting is **reveing**
91. Widely used method of mounting in commercial fishing - **reveing**
92. The process of fitting the necessary ropes and accumulation to make net ready for fishing is **rigging**
93. The knot used for connecting the two lines called **bend**
94. Knot used to join the bent to other line - **hitch**
95. **Reef knot** are used to bending the equal size rope
96. **Splicing** is a method of joining the two rope
97. The process of repairing the damaged net is called as **mending**
98. **Von Brandt** - 1972 classification is the most popular one and universal accepted
99. The technique of catching fish with hand lines and ripping hooks is called **pilking** or **jigging**
100. Surface in trap is called as **aerial**
101. Flying fish are caught in **scoop net** al trap
102. **Gapes net without wings** also known as **stow net**
103. **Double stick seine nets** are more popular with **riverine fisherman**
104. **Ring net** is a hybrid type Lampara and purse seine
105. Hand lift net are used to catch the **crab**
106. Chinese lift net operated in the principle of **lever**
107. Pump fishing became popular for **squid**
108. Kaichund – **Kerala**
109. Borahi&barandajal – **Orissa**
110. Charpattijal – **West Bengal**
111. Waghu, asu, kavi - Maharashtra
112. Mal jalo, jano - Orissa
113. Bandal – **Utrapradesh**

114. A pipe webbing is attached to the fore part of the cod end to prevent the escape of fish – **flapper**
115. An old piece of webbing called (apron) is attached to the below the cod end as a **chaffing gear**
116. In four seam trawler the triangular piece of webbing known as **jibs**
117. In two seam trawler the triangular piece of webbing is known as **dog ear**
118. Bull rope attached between head line and cod end known as **lazy line** or **poop line, pork line**
119. Otter boat are used to keep the mouth of the trawl net **horizontal opening**
120. **Pennant** used to connect a ring on the back side of the otter board
121. Prior to introduction of otter trawl, the **trawl beam** are used
122. Bull trawling also known as **pair trawling**
123. In Spain bull trawl known as **Pareja trawling**
124. The otter board used are mainly of the **suberkrub type**
125. The mid water trawl also known as **pelagic trawl**, floating trawl, **Larsen trawl**
126. Two board mid water trawling was first introduced commercially by Robert Larsen in Denmark 1948
127. In seines fishes accumulated in the **bunt** region
128. In seine portion between the bunt and wing is called as **shoulder**
129. The length of beach seine **150 - 200m & height 5 - 40m**
130. Danish seine was comes under the category of the **boat seine**
131. Fly dragging also known as **Scottish seine**
132. Lampara net has dust **pan shape**
133. End part of the seine is known as **wing**
134. In seine triangular piece of webbing at wing end called **choke**
135. The ropes connecting each purse seine ring with the foot rope are called as **ring bridles**
136. **Seven** basic purse seine system are available
137. The most common type of purse seining method in **western one boat system**
138. South African Lampara system used to exploit the **pilchard and mackerel fisheries**
139. Tuna long lines are firstly operated in the tuticorin in **1963 in india**

140. **Japan pioneered** the introduction of tuna long line
141. Troll line are popular for **salmon and tuna** in California
142. In India troll line are operated In the **Lakshadweep only**
143. In troll lines operation lines are towed at a speed of **4 - 6 knots**
144. **Miyamoto** established the horse power of engine and size of the trawl net
145. The size of the trawl net is usually determined by the **length of the head rope**
146. The length of the trawl net is **1.1 - 1.5** times the head rope length
147. Fish trawl net has varying mesh size about **5 - 20 mm**
148. Shrimp trawler have smaller mesh size ranging from 4-5 mm
149. **Suberkrubs** otter boards finds extensive use in mid water trawls
150. The relationship between the mesh bar and the length of the fish to be caught established by the **Baranov**
151. Hanging coefficient for both Gilling and entangling is **0.5**

31

Fishing Technology

1. Examples of grappling gears – **Clamps, Tongs and Raking devices**.
2. Wounding gears with sharp projectiles – **Spears, Lances, Fish plummets, Fish comb, Arrows, Harpoons, Blow guns, Rifles**.
3. **Brail net** – Large scoop net.
4. **Jerk net** – a rectangular net kept under tension between two sticks which are pushed forward.
5. Collection of shells and corals for decoration and small fishes for aquarium is called as **Aesthetic fishing**.
6. Fish plummets are also called as **plume lines or plumed lines**.
7. The cross section of the two seam trawl during operation is **elliptical**.
8. **Bridles** – legs of trawl.
9. **Sweep lines** serve as **false netting** under water and vibrate in the water column.
10. The size of the trawl net is generally referred by the **length of the head rope**.
11. **Jibs** – Wedges or Quarters (triangular piece of webbing attached to the either side of the upper and lower bellies at their junction).
12. **Bosom** – the **middle portion** of the trawl net between the wings.
13. **Square** – overhang.
14. **Throat** – **extension piece** or lengthener.
15. **Top wedge** – found only in **four seam trawl**.
16. Side wedge – longitudinal piece of webbing seamed between the upper and lower belly on the both sides.
17. Flapper – funnel, pocket, value, trap.
18. Apron – dress.
19. **Selvedge** – meshes made of **thicker twine** than the rest of webbing.

20. **Bolch line** – rope of strong construction to which the webbing is initially hung.
21. **Lacing twine** – a thin strong twine used for seaming the **longitudinal edges** of the webbing.
22. **Tickler chain** – attached to the foot **rope of a trawl** to disturb the bottom.
23. Bobbins – **Rollers**.
24. **Miyamato** (1959) evolved the empirical formulae for the design of a four seam non-over hanging trawl.
25. The length of leg is usually **1/ 5th**of the head rope length.
26. **Dheen leno** or Dan-le-nos are strong shorty sticks or iron pieces attached to the end of either **wings of the trawl** to keep wing tips stretched vertically.
27. Small winged bags of netting held between two sticks are called as **baby seine nets**.
28. **Lampara nets** are traditional Egyptian fishing gear widely used in Nile Delta for **sardine fishery**.
29. The term 'lampara' comes from Greek language which means 'Lamp'.
30. **Lampara** net is a true surrounding pelagic gear.
31. Lampara net looks like a **dust pan provided** with wings.
32. Purse rings – **oval shape**.
33. **Bunt** – region in purse seine net where the catch accumulated before brailing.
34. Purse seine encircling is done within **4 to 8 minutes** for large seines takes **15 to 20** minutes..
35. The maximum pursing speed **(2m/ s)** depends on the power and the speed of the winch.
36. In India, purse seines are **operated** along **west coast** and have been **banned in east** coast.
37. **Shot** – single piece of net in a **fleet**.
38. **Brace line** – used for lacing the adjoining shots in a fleet prior to operation.
39. **Bobbing** is a type of line fishing performed **without hooks** (bait lines).
40. **Gorges** – safety device **fixed with prey** to prevent the escape of fish.
41. Simplest form of line fishing gear is the **hand line**.

42. **Long lines** are used to capture pelagic and demersal fishes of high economic value.
43. **Gangen – branch line** by which a hook or bait are attached to the main line of a long line.
44. Troll line – **active gear**.
45. Troll line is called as **trawl line in U.S.A**.
46. **Japanese fishermen** were the first to use light for fishing squid with jigging lines.
47. One jigging line carries up to **30 jigs**.
48. The power requirement for one jigging machine is about **½ HP** and electric drive of about **220 V** is also used.
49. Trammel net – **French** word – Trois mollies.
50. Cast net – **conical** in shape during **operation**.
51. In India, aluminium floats are made up of **14 - gauge Aluminium** – Manganese alloy.
52. Wooden floats are coated with coal tar to prevent absorption of water.
53. Thermocole floats **cannot** withstand in **high pressure**.
54. **Sponge** floats are not suited for trawl net because of its **poor pressure resistance**.
55. Glass floats are operated even at the depth more than **200 fathoms**.
56. Glass floats are used in **long lines** and as **marker buoys** in seine nets.
57. The steel floats are **quickly rusted**.
58. **Sinkers** are used to keep the net at **desired depth**.
59. **Buoys** are used as **marking aid** in fishing operation.
60. Anchor is used to keep the fleet in position at sea by chaining it to the sea bottom.
61. **Shackle** is semi-circular bar of metal used for **fastening** the parts together.
62. **Thimble** is called as **eye of the rope**.
63. **Swivel** is used to prevent **twists and kinks**.
64. **Suberkrub** otter boards are originally developed for **bottom trawling**.
65. Capstan (slow turning) and line haulers (fast turning) are small and simple winches used for turning.

32

Biochemical Techniques and Instrumentation

1. **Chromatography** – Technique for the separation of one or more biological compounds from the mixture.
2. Chromatography – **Mikhail Tswett** (1906)
3. Distribution or **partial coefficient** is defined as the ratio of concentration of compounds in the mobile phase to that the concentration of compounds in the stationary phase.
4. Chromatography – also used for the **separation of the colorless** compounds from a mixture.
5. **Spectroscopy** employs the interaction of light with matter.
6. Light is electromagnetic radiation (EMR) that exhibit discrete packets of energy is called as **photons**.
7. Jablonski diagram gives the electronic and vibrational state of the molecule.
8. Molecular structures responsible for the interaction with EMR are called as **Chromophores**.
9. **Beer's law** is valid for **low** concentrations only.
10. Prism splits incoming light into its components by refraction.
11. Grating splits the wavelengths by diffraction.
12. Monochromator consists of either a prism or a rotating metal grind of high precision called as gratings.
13. Photomultipier tube is sensitive than photocells.
14. Rf value = Relative factor value (ratio of distance moved by solute to the distance moved by solvent front.
15. Rf value is always constant for a particular compound under standard conditions.
16. Ligand must specifically bind to one particular compound.
17. Spacer arm interposed between ligand and matrix.

18. Gel filtration chromatography – invented by Grant Henry Lathe and Colin R Ruthven.
19. Jerker Porath and Per Floding introduced dextran gels.
20. Size of Coarse gel **100 - 300 µm**.
21. Size of fine gel **20 - 80 µm**.
22. Cross-linked dextrans – **Sephadex**.
23. Agarose – **Sepharose, Bio Gel A**.
24. Polyacrylamide – **Bio Gel P**.
25. Polyacryloyl morphine – Enzocryl gel.
26. Polystyrene – Bio Beads S.
27. Molecular size exclusion limit of dextran gel is 200-800 Kilo Dalton.
28. Molecular size exclusion limit of polyacrylamide gel is 1.8 to 400 Kilo Dalton.
29. Molecular size exclusion limit of porous glass gravels is 3000 to 9 million Dalton.
30. IEC – Ion Exchange Chromatography.
31. Cation exchangers – negatively charged groups.
32. Anion exchangers – positively charged groups.
33. Packing resin in IEC – Polystyrene, Cellulose, Polyacrylate and Agarose.
34. Strong exchangers – Sulphonate ($-SO_3$) and Quaternary ammonium compounds ($-N^+R_3$).
35. Weak exchangers – Carboxylate (-COO) and Diethylammonium ($-HN^+(CH_2CH_3)_2$.
36. German Fritz Prior – Invented Gas Solid Chromatography.
37. Archer JP Martin – Invented Gas Liquid Chromatography.
38. Volume of packed column – **1 to 5 µl**.
39. Volume of capillary column – **0.5 µl**.
40. In GC, the splitter is used to deliver a fraction of injection 1:50 to 1:500.
41. In GC, the split ratio is controlled by adjusting flow through split vent.
42. In GC, the flow rate is measured by gas bubble flow meter.
43. In GC, the column materials are made up of Glass, Stainless or Teflon – Packed column.
44. In GC, the column materials are made up of metal, plastic glass and fused silica – Capillary column.

45. SCOT columns are less efficient than WCOT columns.
46. WCOT – Wall Coated Open Tubular column.
47. SCOT – Support Coated Open Tubular column.
48. FSOT – Fused Silica Open Tubular column.
49. PLOT – Porous layer Open Tubular column.
50. Polyethylene glycol adepic acid – Carbowax.
51. Polysiloxanes – OV, SE, XE.
52. Detectors detect and quantify the components eluted from the column.
53. Detectors produce response proportional to component that is separated by column.
54. FLD – Flame ionization Detector.
55. ELD – Electron Capture Detector.
56. FPD – Flame Photometric Detector.
57. TCD – Thermal Conductivity Detector.
58. PID – Photo Ionization Detector.
59. FIDs are mass sensitive rather than concentration sensitive.
60. FID is a universal detector for the analysis of organic compounds.
61. ECD – highly sensitive.
62. FPD – selectively detects phosphorus and sulphur compounds.
63. Amplifier receives an output from a detector and amplifies it so that the signal can be detected by a recorder or integrator.
64. Integrator takes signal from amplifier and produces an output (chromatogram) and peak height or area of quantification.
65. Radio immuno assay technique was invented by **Berson & yallow**
66. ELISA invented by peter Permian & Eva Engvall -1971

33

Marine Engineering

1. 1 Kilo joule – **10^3 joule**.
2. 1 Mega joule – **10^6 joule**.
3. 1 Kilowatt hour – **$3.6*10^6$ joule**.
4. The heat engine converts heat energy into **mechanical energy**.
5. The machine which converts one forms of energy to another form is called as **engine** or **prime mover**.
6. **Fahrenheit scale** is called as British thermal unit and denoted by B.Th.U.
7. Internal combustion engines using coal gas as fuel was made by **Frenchman Etienne Lenoir (1860)**.
8. Silent gas engine was developed by Germans **Nileolansotto & Eugen Langen**.
9. **Rudolph diesel** made the first diesel engine in 1894.
10. TDC is also called as **inner dead centre**.
11. BDC is also called as **outer dead centre**.
12. **Stroke** is the distance through which the piston moves from TDC to BDC inside the cylinder.
13. The inner diameter of the working cylinder is called the **cylinder bore**.
14. Total volume = **Swept volume + Clearance volume**.
15. Compression ratio for diesel engine = **16:1 to 20:1**.
16. Compression ratio for petrol engine = **7:1 to 10:1**.
17. **Suction stroke** = piston moves from TDC to BDC.
18. **Compression stroke** = piston moves from BDC to TDC.
19. Empirical formula for mean effective pressure is **PLAN/ 4500**.
20. Major heat loss is through **exhaust**.
21. $\text{Thermal efficiency} = \dfrac{\text{heat converted into useful work}}{\text{total heat supplied}}$

22. $\text{Mechanical efficiency} = \frac{\text{Brake Horse Power}}{\text{Indicated Horse Power}}$

23. $\text{Volumetric Efficiency} = \frac{\text{Volume of air actually drawn inside the cylinder}}{\text{Theoretical volume of air the cylinder can hold}}$

24. The structural base of the engine formed by **bed plate**.
25. The longitudinal and transverse plate of engine is called as **girders**.
26. **Side clearance** is the clearance of the **piston ring** and **ring grove** on the piston.
27. End clearance is also called as **butt clearance**.
28. The pin which connects small end of connecting rod with piston is called **Gudgeon** pin or piston pin.
29. The rod transmits the motion of cam to the rocker arm is called as **push rod**.
30. **Exhaust manifold** collects the burned gases from each cylinder.
31. **Silencer** is used to **reduce the sound** of the engine.
32. Daily service tank is also called as **day tank**.
33. Specific gravity of diesel ranging from **0.8 – 0.99**.
34. **Weight of the fuel** = volume of fuel * specific gravity of the fuel.
35. **Marine engine** uses a **low viscous diesel** or heavy residual diesel.
36. The fluctuation of the speed from the set point speed is called **hunting**.
37. **Snap tank** mainly used for **calculating the late of flow** of fuel to the engine.
38. **Flow meter** is a meter used to measure the fuel consumption to a marine diesel engine.
39. $\text{Brake fuel consumption} = \frac{\text{fuel consumption / hour}}{\text{brake horse power}}$
40. Starting point of solidification is called **cloud point**.
41. Cam wheel is also called as **cog wheel**.
42. Scavenge fire takes place in **2 stroke engine**.
43. 1 watt = 1 joule per second.
44. 1 horse power = **746 watts**.
45. 1 kilowatt = **1.3405 horse power**.
46. **Fixed pitch** and **variable pitch** propeller are the two types of propeller found.

47. **Pocker gauge** is an instrument used to measure **propeller drop**.
48. **Dammel gauge** is an instrument used to measure **rudder drop**.
49. First patent for OBM was taken in **France** (1860).
50. First commercial model of **OBM** was available in America.
51. Sweden introduced the French "MOTOGODILL" in 1907 which is nick named as "POWER RUDDER".
52. Propeller co-efficient of fishing vessel is **0.15 to 0.3**.
53. Dry corrosion is also called as **Scaling or tarnishing**.
54. The shroud or cover plate of impeller is called as **crown plate**.
55. Blasting concentrating only on particular rusted area is known as **spot blasting**.
56. Clearance volume also called as **compression volume**
57. **Compression ratio** the ratio between total volume and the clearance volume
58. The fuel is sprayed inside the cylinder by the **injector & air by blower**
59. In **two stroke** engines instead of valves. The **ports** are available
60. In two stroke petrole engine early period of upward stroke the **fresh air get into the cylinder**
61. In two stroke engines. the later period of the upward stroke is a **compression stroke**
62. The first half of downward stroke is a **power stroke**
63. **Main bearing** is used to hold the crankshaft on the axis its rotation
64. The crank case is also called as **sump**
65. The trunk piston consist of **crown**
66. **Bunkering** is the process of taking fuel in vessel
67. **Sounding** is the process of measuring the quantity of oil present in the main tank
68. Sounding done by **sounding tap**.

Fisheries Extension Economics and Statistics

34

Fisheries Administration

1. **Luther Gullick** denoted the functional elements of the administration **POSDCORB**.
2. CIFNET – Central Institute of Fisheries Nautical Engineering and Training. It was started in **1963**. The head quarters situated in **cochin**.
3. CIFNET have **two units** .one **Chennai**, another one **Visag**.
4. IFP –integrated fishery project was started in **1952**.
5. During 2008 the FPT was renamed as **NIFPHTT**. It has situated in **cochin**.
6. FSI- fishery survey of India. It has head quarter in **Mumbai**.
7. CICEF- Central Institute of Coastal Engineering for Fishery. It is situated in **Bangalore**.
8. CICEF was renamed in **1983** as PISFH –pre investment of fishing harbor
9. NFDB –national fisheries development board .established in **2006**. It has head quarters in **Hyderabad**.
10. CAA-coastal aquaculture authority established **in 2005**. It has head quarter in **Chennai**.
11. Coastal zone regulation notification - **1991**.
12. Indian forest act **1927**. its amendment act **1984**.
13. Forest Conservation Act - **1980**.
14. The national environmental appellate authority act **1997**.
15. EEZ & other maritime zone **act 1976**.
16. The Coast Guard Act - **1978**.
17. Indian Port Act - **1908**.
18. Guidelines for fishing operation of **Indian EEZ** in 2002.
19. Environmental protection **act 1986**.
20. Indian wild life act **1972**. its amendment act in **2002**.

21. The water prevention and control act - **1974**.
22. Biological Diversity Act - **2002**.
23. Comprehensive Marine Fishing Policy - **2004**.
24. Tamil Nadu Marine Fishing Regulation Act – **1983**.
25. MPEDA – Marine Product Export Development Agency in 1972. its comes under **Ministry of Commerce** (16/ 08/ 1972).
26. Wetland (RAMSAR) Convention - **1972**.
27. CITES – Convention on International Trade in Endangered species of flora and fauna - **1973**.
28. CBD- Convention on Biological Diversity - **1992**.
29. Convention on the Conservation of Migratory Species (CMS) of wild life animals - **1979**.
30. India adapted UNCLOS-united nation convention on law of the sea - **1982**.
31. India develop its first marine fishing policy during **10th five year plan**.
32. **DARE** - Department of Agriculture Research and Education.
33. Factories Act - **1948**.
34. Land Reforms Act - **1974**. its amendment act **1995**.
35. National Environmental Policy - **2006**.
36. Merchant Shipping Act - **1958**.
37. EIA – Export Inspection Act in **1963**.
38. Foreign Trade Act - **1992**.
39. Karnataka Marine Fishing Regulation Act - **1986**.
40. FSSAI - Food Safety Standard Authority Act of India - **2006**.
41. Ecologically Sensitive Area comes under the **CRZ 1 (I)**.
42. Area between LTL to HTL comes under **CRZ 1 (II)**.
43. CRZ 3- No Development Area.
44. Marine fishing regulation act - **1981**.
45. FAO established in **1945**.
46. The Indian ocean tuna commission - **1996 - 97**.
47. CCAMLR – Commission for the Conservation of Antarctic Marine Living Resources - **1982**.
48. APFIC - Asian Pacific Fisheries Commission by FAO in **1948**.
49. **BIMSTEC** - Bay of Bengal Initiative for multi-sectoral technical & economic corporation started in 1997.

50. BOBP – **2003** (Bay of Bengal Programme).
51. INFOFISH was originally launched in **1981 by FAO**.
52. **SAARC** - South Asian Association for Regional Cooperation - 1985.
53. Hazards Waste Management Act - **1989**.
54. Deep Sea Fishing Policy - **1991**.
55. National Environmental Tribunal Act - **1995.**
56. Environmental Impact Assessment Notification in - **1994**.
57. Land Acquisition Act **1894**.
58. Father of public administration **Woodrow Wilson**.
59. CIBA established in **7th five** year plan during - **1987**.
60. CIFA established in 1987 at Odisha.
61. CIFE established in **1961**.
62. CIFT established in **1957** at Kochi.
63. NBFGR – National Bureau of Fish Genetic Resources; established in1983 at **Allahabad** and later shifted into **Lucknow**.
64. NRCCWF – National Research Centre on Cold Water Fisheries; established in **1986;** then it is shifted to Bhimtal in **1997 (DCFR)**.
65. **NCDC** – National Cooperative Development Corporation.
66. FISHCOPED – National FEDERATION of fisherman cooperative limited.
67. FISHCOPED - started in **1982**.
68. MATSYAFED present in **Kerala**.
69. **KGS** - Knowledge Generating System.
70. **KDS** - Knowledge Disseminating System.
71. **KCS** - Knowledge Communication System.
72. NDP - National Demonstration Project - **1965.**
73. **ORP** - Operational Research Project.
74. LLP- Lab to Land Product - **1979**.
75. KVK & TTC - **1974.**
76. Institute of Village Linkage Programme (IVLP) - **1997**.
77. FFDA- started in **1973 - 74**.
78. Pacific Halibut Commission - **1953**.
79. International Whaling Commission - **1946**.

35

Disaster Management

1. The most disaster affected populations in the world – China.
2. Heavy droughts usually occur in Afghanistan.
3. Heavy human causalities due to flood occur in Cambodia.
4. Ring of fire – an arc of volcanoes and fault lines encircling the Pacific basin.
5. Occurrence of unusual cold wave – Russia.
6. 22 Indian states are prone to disasters.
7. Pre-Disaster mitigation can help in ensuring faster recovery from impacts of disaster.
8. IOC – International Oceanographic Commission.
9. USGS – United States Geological Survey.
10. NOAA – National Oceanic and Atmospheric Administrations.
11. IOTWSP – Indian Ocean Tsunami Warning System Program.
12. DART – Deep Ocean Assessment and Reporting of Tsunami.
13. PMEL – Pacific Marine Environmental Laboratory.
14. NIOSH – National Institute of Occupational Safety and Health (USA).
15. NBRO – National Building Research Organisation.
16. MD – Meteorological Department.
17. ID – Irrigation Department.
18. CBDP – Community Based Disaster Preparedness.
19. NDMC – National Disaster Management Centre.
20. ISDR – International Strategy for Disaster Reduction.
21. 36 million people – engaged in fishing and fish farming activities.
22. 15 million people – employed aboard decked.
23. Pollution is the beginning of a waste into the atmosphere.
24. Pollution is the life killer but also a life safer.

25. Technology is act as a cleaner to preserve earth.
26. Water has made earth poles apart from planets.
27. Activities actually eliminate or reduce the probability of disaster occurrence is known as Mitigation.
28. Speed of Tsunami waves – 500 to 1000 km/h.
29. Risk Assessment helps in identification and collection of information about the hotspot areas.
30. Vulnerability analysis helps in determining the intensity and time taken for the recovery of the impact by disaster.

36

Fisheries Extension

1. The word Extension was first used in **U.S.A**.
2. The word Extension is derived from **Latin** meaning out stretching.
3. Extension education = **non formal education**.
4. **Extension work** = out of school system of education.
5. **Learning** = active process on the part of the learner.
6. Motivation = need satisfy goal-seeking behaviour.
7. Steps in extension teaching methods = **AIDCAS**.
8. **Teaching** is the process of providing situations in which learning takes place.
9. **Learning** is the process by which a person becomes changes in his behaviour through **self-activity**.
10. **Lecture** is the best method for presenting information to large number of persons in a short period of time.
11. **Panel is an informal** conversation before audience by a selected group of persons under a moderator.
12. Types of panels are **question-answer, set speech** and **conversational panel**.
13. Huddle method is also known as discussion **66 or Philips 66**.
14. Newest idea is called as **brain trust**.
15. Role playing is the dramatization of a problem or a situation in the general area human relations.
16. **Workshop** = one day to several weeks.
17. **Conference** is a pooling of experiences and opinions among a group of people who have special qualifications in an area.
18. **Mass teaching** methods = **exhibition**, radio talk, motion pictures, slide shows and printed materials.
19. **Radio talk** is the quickest way of communicating technical information and innovations to the fishermen.
20. **Campaign** is a well organised plan for bringing about widespread adoption of a particular practice.

21. **Flyer** (leaflet) is a single sheet of paper used to present information on only one topic in a simple language.
22. The size of the leaflet is **4 "X 8"**.
23. Pamphlet = 2 to 12 pages.
24. Bulletin = **12 to 20 pages**.
25. Booklet = **exceeds 20 pages** and limited within 50 pages.
26. Book = **exceeds 50 pages**.
27. 5 rules for the creation of posters are: theme, psychology, wording, composition of design and colour management.
28. Charts make learning experiences more **vivid and long lasting**.
29. A flannel graph or board is a very handy aid to extension workers.
30. **Indirect projection system** = OHP.
31. **OHP** = Over Head Projector.
32. Reflected projection = Epidiascope / opaque projector.
33. For **opaque projector**, the actual projectable material should not exceed **10 "X 10"**.
34. The characteristics that determine innovation's rate of adoption are relative advantage, compatibility, complexity, trial ability and observability.
35. Innovators = 2.5%
36. Early adapters = 13.5%
37. Early majority = 34%
38. Late majority = 34%
39. Laggards = 16%
40. The stages of **adoption process** are awareness, interest, evaluation, trail and adoption.
41. **Decision** is a word derived from **Latin** means off to cut.
42. Steps in innovation decision process = knowledge, persuasion, decision, implementation and confirmation.
43. **Colloque** is a gathering at which a panel of individual discuss a subject in front of an audience.
44. **Fact sheet** is a publication of six pages on a single subject of a component of a broader topic.
45. **Study kit** is a collection of educational materials created on a specific subject.

37

Fisheries Marketing

1. A good market always serves to safeguard the interest of the trader and the consumer.
2. The core fish marketing system is classified the three types as **market penetration, market development and products development**.
3. **College of Mangalore** developed technology for **fish sausages**.
4. **CIFE Mumbai** developed technology to manufacture **fish wafers**.
5. Mandala committee – Gujarat.
6. **Aratdars** is commonly called as Commission agent.
7. Selling is also done by **contract method**.
8. Concentric diversification – the products have technological and marketing synergies with the existing fish commodity sale.
9. **Horizontal diversification** – adding new product to the present products.
10. **Conglomerate diversification** – it is a firm seeking add new commodities to new classes of customers because this will set some of the deficiencies of old products.
11. Co-operative marketing in Orissa was introduced in 1949-50 in the Chilka Lake.
12. Monopoly – only one seller.
13. **Bilateral monopoly** – presence of single **seller** and single **buyer**.
14. Duopoly – presence of two dominant sellers.
15. Oligopoly – competition among few sellers.
16. **Pure** oligopoly – presence of small number of sellers selling homogenous but **not** closely substitutable products.
17. Differentiated oligopoly – the presence of few dominant sellers selling slightly **differentiated products**.
18. **Monopolistic** competition – has **both perfect competition** and **monopoly** markets.
19. **Monopsony** – only one regular buyer.

20. **Monopsonistic** competition – presence of a fairly large number of buyers buying slightly **differentiated** products.
21. **Monopolistic** competition exists in the **small fish landing** centres.
22. **Oligopsony** market exists in the **medium fish landing centres**.
23. **Oligopoly** market situation exist in **freshwater fish marketing** because of the presence of few sellers.
24. In **freshwater fish marketing** from **buyers** point of view, **oligopsony** market condition exists because of the presence of few dominant buyers.
25. **Marketing channels** – route through which goods and services are moved from place of production to the place of consumption.
26. The channel efficiency can be determined by formula:

    ME = (MM/MC) +1

    a) ME: Marketing Efficiency of a channel distribution

    b) MM: Marketing Margin per Consignment

    c) MC: Marketing Cost per Consignment
27. **Huegy and Mitchell** (1957) classified the marketing functions from the economic point of view.
28. The most widely accepted definition for marketing functions was given by **Clark and Clark in 1947**.
29. **Exchange functions** –Assembling,.Buying and selling.
30. **Physical** supply functions – Transportation, Storage and warehousing.
31. **Facilitating** functions – Standardisation, Grading, Financing, Risk bearing and market information.
32. **Buying** is the **first** step of marketing functions.
33. Pyle defines the term of buying in the market.
34. The elements of buying include determination of demand, locating sources of supply, assembling, negotiation and contract of purchase.
35. **Buying by inspection** is a method adopted by the **wholesalers**.
36. Assembling involves gathering and monitoring stocks by different preservation methods purchased from different sources.
37. **Quotations** called for the closed tender systems.
38. Marine fish landing centres follows **open auction system**.
39. Storage is defined as the method of preservation of goods between the time of production and the time of consumption.
40. Standardisation means the establishment of certain standards of both quantity and quality.

41. The risk bearing function is accepting the possibility of loss in the marketing of a product.
42. Types of risks: physical risk and market risk.
43. **Market risks** occur due to changes in product price, demand and supply.
44. Merchant middlemen – **Wholesaler and retailer**.
45. Speciality wholesalers carry restricted products by using a part of marketing channel.
46. **Retailers** provide **linkage** between the wholesalers and the consumers.
47. Retailers is a merchant whose **main business selling directly** to the consumers.
48. Agent middlemen do not take the title of the ownership of goods.
49. Types of commission agent – C.A. Purchase and C.A. Sales.
50. Price spread – producer's share in consumer's rupee.
51. **A good pricing policy** helps to achieve **maximum sales revenue**.
52. **Price** can decide the success or failure of a frim.
53. Profit maximisation can be achieved when monopolistic competition exists in the market.
54. **Internal factors** that affecting pricing decisions are organisational factors, marketing mix, product differentiation, product cost and firm's objectives.
55. **External factors** that affecting pricing decisions are demand, competition, suppliers, buyers and economic conditions.
56. Pricing policies provide the framework and consistency needed by the firm to make reasonable and effective pricing decisions.
57. Basic pricing policies are cost, demand and competition oriented pricing policy.
58. Mark up pricing is also called as **cost plus pricing**.
59. A high introductory price is fixed in the initial stage of the product introduced in the market is known as **skimming price**.
60. Negotiated pricing is also called as **variable pricing**.
61. There Are 6 types of promotion mix found.
62. **Publicity** – non-personal stimulation of demand for a product.
63. **Public relation** – most powerful tool to develop an image about the product.
64. **Advertising** – any paid form of non-personal communication of ideas and products.

65. Market segmentation is the division of a market into groups of segments having similar wants.
66. Sales promotion techniques are also known as by the names of **extra purchase value**.
67. Product planning and positioning can be explained by using a **product positioning map**.
68. **Organisation** is the process of establishing relationship.
69. The organisational relationship is in the form of authority and responsibility.
70. Existing problems in marine marketing are as follows, perishability, price uncertainty, swiftness in auctioning process, lack of marketing infrastructure and protracted payment by the buyers.
71. India ranks **third** in the world in the **total fish production** and **second** in **inland** aquaculture.
72. Fisheries sector contributes **1.01 - 1.45%** to GDP.
73. The overall fish production in the country at present is 7.85 million tonnes of which 3.32 million tonnes contributed by marine sector.
74. Fishermen's share in consumer's rupee ranges from 47.5 to 82.7% of various varieties of fish.
75. **SEETTD** – Socio Economic Evaluation and Technology Transfer Division.
76. **ASEAN** – Association of South East Asian Nations.
77. **FDWC** – Fishermen Development and Welfare Co-operative Societies.
78. **FISHCOOPFED** – National Federation of Fishermen's Co-operative.
79. **FMSP** – Fisheries Management Science Program.
80. **ICSF** – International Collective in Support of Fish Workers.
81. **NSDP** – Net State Domestic Product.
82. **NSSO** – National Sample Survey Organisation.
83. **SHG** – Self Help Group.
84. **TBT** – Technical Barriers to Trade.
85. **TNFDC** – Tamil Nadu Fisheries Development Corporation Ltd.
86. **RP** – Retail Price.
87. **LP** – Landing centre Price.
88. Marketing relates to the creation of all the **four utilities**.
89. **Selling** relates only to the creation of **possession utility**.

90. Developing and presenting a new product at right time create **form utility**.
91. **Place utility** is created where goods and services are available at places where **they are needed**.
92. Objective behind the creation of the utilities is to **achieve profit**.
93. Definition of marketing is explained by **Philip Kotler** and Gary Armstrong (core marketing concept).
94. Consumer's choice – Judgement on product's value.
95. Form utility – **Processing functions**.
96. Time utility – **Storage in Warehouses**.
97. Place utility – **Transportation**.
98. Possession Utility – Ownership/ Satisfaction of human needs or wants.
99. *Mercatus* – to trade; meaning – merchandise (place of business).
100. **Trade** refers to a negotiation between two parties for a **mutual benefit**.
101. **Commerce** – any exchange of commodity.
102. **Merchandising** refers to act of selling.
103. Marketing = Trade + Commerce + Merchandising.
104. **Retail market** is last link the channel of distribution.
105. An **organisational characteristic** of market is known as **market structure**.
106. The determination of **output** and **prices** are affected by the market structure.
107. Market structure influences the nature of **competition and pricing**.
108. Fisheries products – **Perishable distinctiveness**.
109. Theprocess by which the distinctiveness gradually disappears as the product merges with other competitive products is termed as "the cycle of competitive degeneration".
110. **Pricing** – Maximum sales revenue.
111. Any object or device which carry advertisement message is called **advertisement medium (AM)**.
112. AM – used for conveying advertisement message to consumers.
113. Substantiality refers to the size of segmented markets.
114. Principle of market segmentation – **"Ability to buy"**.
115. Sales promotion – **Extra Purchase Value**.
116. **Field work** – data collection.

117. Market penetration increases sales in existing market.
118. Product planning can be explained by **product positioning map**.
119. **Exploratory research** – preliminary research help to define problem and suggest hypothesis.
120. **Descriptive research** – demographic features and attitudes of consumers.
121. Casual research – **Test hypotheses**.
122. "Dhalta" system – aratdar's take 2.5kg of fish for every 50kg of fish sold.
123. The first co-operative society was established by a group of weavers at Toadlane Rochdale in U.K. (1844).
124. In fisheries sector, the first co-operative society was established in India at **Maharashtra** ("KARLA MACHHIMAR") during **1913**.
125. Saving cum relief scheme **-1991 to 1992**.
126. BFDA, FFDA, MPEDA – provide financial support for fish or shrimp farming besides technical and extension support.
127. NABARD, NCDC – provide funds for developing the farming activities.
128. Commercial and co-operative banks – provide short/ long term loans for the fish farmers.
129. 1st five year plan was started during 1951-1956.
130. ATR method – Product based consumer awareness.
131. Co-operative planning committee – 1946.
132. Roachdalepoineers made first aim to establish co-operatives.
133. NCDC – 1974.
134. FISHCOPFED – 1980.
135. National level co-operative – 1.
136. State level co-operatives in India – 17.
137. Central level co-operatives in India – 108.
138. Primary level co-operatives in India – 11440.
139. Members of co-operatives in India – 125 million.
140. Indian co-operative movement – 1904.
141. FMS – Focus Market Scheme.
142. AAS – Advance Authorization Scheme.
143. EPCG – Export Promotion Capital Goods Scheme.
144. TEE – Towns of export excellence.
145. MAI – Market Access Initiative.
146. RCMC – Registration Cum Membership Certificate.

38

Fisheries Project Management

1. **Project monitoring** is an integral part of project management.
2. Concurrent evaluation is carried out during **implementation of the project**.
3. Terminal evaluation is undertaken at the time of **completion of the project**.
4. **Ex-post** evaluation is also called as **impact evaluation**.
5. **Network techniques** are used for **minimising cost and time** of the project.
6. **PERT** – Program Evaluation and Review Technique.
7. **LOT** – Latest Occurrence Time.
8. **CPM** – Critical Path Method.
9. Project presentation – 30 pages.
10. National level project – goal of economic growth.
11. Sectoral level project – sectoral development.
12. The **analysis of costs and benefits** of a project are called as **appraisal**.
13. Costs and benefits of a projects measure in terms of price and market: cash flow.
14. **Rate of interest decreases** – project will not worth – **cut off rate**.
15. Price paid for any factor of production in fixed supply – **rent**.
16. Study of **odds** of the project is called as **risk analysis**.
17. **Shadow price** is modified market price to correctly reflect the true value of inputs and outputs.
18. Income forgone in the alternative use – opportunity cost.
19. Compounding = PS $(1+r)^n$.
20. Discounting = FS $[1/(1+r)^n]$.
21. $\text{Simple Rate of Returns} = \frac{\text{Average Annual Net Benefits}}{\text{Initial Investments}} * 100$.

22. $\text{Payback period} = \frac{\text{Initial Investments}}{\text{Verage Annual Net Benefits}}$.
23. Net present value = PVNB - II (netted method).
24. Net Present value = PVTB - PVTC (aggregate method).
25. $\text{Benefit cost ratio} = \frac{\text{PVBB}}{11}$ (netted mettod).
26. $\text{Benefit cost ratio} = \frac{\text{PVTB}}{\text{PVTC}}$ (aggregate method).
27. Project cost and benefits are affected by **risk and uncertainty**.
28. NPV gives an absolute measure of benefits in terms of rupees.
29. BCR gives a measure of benefits per rupee of investment.
30. IRR obtains at a rate of discount where **NPV = 0; BCR = 1**.
31. Project formulation – multi-disciplinary effort.
32. Project definition was given by Price **Gittinger** (1986).
33. Fisheries investment project definition was given by **Campleman** (1976).
34. A sound database is a pre-requisite to the formulation of a good project.
35. Modified definition of costs and benefits were given by Gregerson&Contreas (1979).
36. Inputs are priced using market price.
37. Benefits arise from increasing the supply of the output.
38. Cash flows involve **time value of money**.
39. Financial analysis is a micro-level appraisal of the project.
40. Financial statement – balance sheet.
41. Total liabilities – **solvency**.
42. Current liabilities – **liquidity**.
43. Dept – equity ratio is the ratio between total liabilities and net worth.
44. Income statement is also called as **profit and loss account**.
45. SCBA – Social Cost Benefit analysis.

39

Fisheries Statistics

1. The word **"Statistics"** derived from the **Latin** word 'Status' meaning POLITICAL STATE.
2. **Statistics** are lifeblood of **successful commerce**.
3. Statistics are **not suitable** to study the **qualitative** phenomenon.
4. Statistics laws are **not exact**.
5. A.L.Bowley – "Statistics are numeral statement of facts in any department of enquiry placed in relation to each other".
6. Croxton and Cowden – "Statistics may be defined as the science of collection, presentation analysis and interpretation of numerical data from the logical analysis".
7. Alfred Marshall – "Statistics are the straw only which I like every other economist has to make the bricks".
8. Function of statistics
   a. Condensation
   b. Comparison
   c. Forecasting
   d. Estimation
   e. Tests of hypothesis
9. ANOVA – **Analysis of Variance**.
10. ANOVA – developed by **Prof. R.A. Fisher**.
11. A finite subset of statistical individual defined in a population is called as a **sample**.
12. The number of units in a sample is called as **sample size**.
13. Random numbers can be generated through **scientific calculator** or **computers**.
14. Simple random sampling is also called as **unrestricted random sampling**.
15. Stratified random sampling is mainly used to **reduce** the population heterogeneity and **increase the efficiency of the estimates**.
16. Widely employed sampling method is **systematic sampling** (Because of its ease and convenience).

17. Systematic sampling is also called as **Quasi - random sampling**.
18. Systematic sampling can be used for **infinite number of samples** (population).
19. The collection of a set of numerical values, collected over a period of time is called as **time series data**.
20. Data collected is connected with that of a place is termed as **spatial data**.
21. Data collected is connected to time as well as place is known as **spacio-temporal data**.
22. Primary data can be collected through
    a. Direct personal interviews
    b. Indirect oral interviews
    c. Information from correspondents
    d. Mailed questionnaire method
    e. Scheduled sent through enumerators
23. Sources of Secondary course of data, classified into
    a. Published sources
    b. Unpublished sources
24. Raw data is also called as **ungrouped data**.
25. Class interval may be defined as the **size of each grouping data**.
26. The difference between the lower and upper class limits is called as **Width or Size** of the class interval.
27. The difference between the largest and smallest value of the observation is called as **Range**.
28. Overlapping of the class intervals is avoided in **inclusive method**.
29. **Diagram** is the visual representation of statistical data, highlighting their basic facts and relationship.
30. **Lorenz curve** is a graphical method of studying **dispersion**.
31. A measure of change in dependent variable with unit change in independent variable – **regression-co-efficient**.
32. X^2 test was developed by – karlpearson
33. **Tugmented design – was developed by** – Federer.
34. F- test was developed by – fisher.
35. Correlation developed by – Cralton
36. Arithmetic mean = sum of all observation / their number

Fisheries Genetics and Biotechnology

40

Fish Biotechnology

1. Biotechnology arises from the field of **Zymotechnology**.
2. The word Biotechnology was coined by **Karl ereky** in 1919.
3. **OECD** – Organisation for Economic Co-operation and Development (1981).
4. National Biotechnology Board – **1982** by GOI.
5. **ICGEB** – International Centre for Genetic Engineering and Bio-technology (1988).
6. **Cohen & Boyer** – Recombinant DNA technology (1973).
7. Restriction enzymes are called as **Molecular scissors**.
8. **Frederick Sanger** – DNA Sequencing techniques.
9. Modified red glow zebra fish came on to the market in **2004**.
10. Tissue culture – **Osowski** 1914.
11. The term molecular biology was used by **Warren weaver**.
12. **Beadle and Tatum** – showed that **genes encode** proteins in 1941.
13. DNA Polymerase was discovered by **Korenberg** in 1957.
14. RNA Polymerase was discovered by **S.Ochoa**.
15. Semi-conservative method of DNA replication was showed by **M. Meselson & F.W. Stahl in 1958**.
16. Nucleic acid hybridization was discovered by **Marmur & Doty** in 1961.
17. Lac operon concept was showed by **F.Jacob & J.Monod** in 1961.
18. Genetic code was deciphered by **M.Nerenberg , H.G.Hora**.
19. Information flow in RNA viruses from RNA to DNA was showed by **H.temin, D.Baltimore**.
20. The first transgenic gold fish was produced by **zhu in 1985**.
21. DNA finger printing was developed by **Alec Jeffry**.
22. First fish gene sequence was reported by **fletcher in 1985**.

23. AFP protein is obtained from – **winter flounder**.
24. A segment of DNA is known as **gene**.
25. Sub unit of DNA and RNA is called as **nucleotide**.
26. The base and sugar joined together called – **nucleoside**.
27. To analyse the 3 dimensional structure of the DNA **X- ray diffraction are used**.
28. The DNA double helix have width size about **2 nm**.
29. RNA as the **genetic material** in the retroviruses.
30. Normal DNA has **2 grooves**.
31. **Z** DNA has **single** groove.
32. A form of DNA contain **11 base pairs**.
33. B form of DNA contain **10 base pairs**.
34. Z form of DNA contain **12 base pairs**.
35. The DNA Contain glycogen and cytosine about **22 - 73 %**.
36. The amount of DNA strand separation is measured by the absorption of DNA solution at the **260 nm**.
37. The higher amount of **G - C content** leads to **higher melting** temperature.
38. To disturb the hydrogen bond between two strand in addition to heating. **DMSO, formamide** also used. Lowering the temperature also.
39. Best temperature for the renaturation of DNA about **25 ^{0}c**.
40. The essential blue print for making protein is – **gene**.
41. The production of protein from a DNA blue print is called **gene expression**.
42. The non-coding section of a DNA act as the initiation site for the mitochondrial DNA replication and transcription that is called as **control region**.
43. The triplet binding test was devised by **Marshall Nirenberg**.
44. Methionine has triplet code – **AUG**.
45. Phenylanine has triplet code – **UUU**.
46. **Stop codons** – UAG, UGA, UAA.
47. The initiation codon is **AUG**.
48. Arginine , Leucine, serine have – **6** different codon.
49. Proline , Alanine have - **4** codon.
50. Isoleusine has - **3 codon**.

51. Methioine and tryptophan have only **one codon**.
52. Whose product are constantly need for the cellular activity known as **house keeping gene**.
53. Those genes are take care of housekeeping function that referred **as constitute**.
54. Each gene segment is referred as **cistron**.
55. Long messenger RNA covering all cistrons is known as **polycistronic**
56. The coding sequences are called **exons**.
57. The interrupting sequences are called **intron**.
58. The process of **ligating** exon together to produce the mature mRNA is called **splicing**.
59. Transcription proceeds from **left to right**.
60. The replication fork is formed with in the nucleus during the **DNA replication**.
61. Coiling of DNA is prevented by enzyme **topoisomerases**.
62. Bacteria have **circular chromosome**.
63. Eukaryotes have **linear chromosome**.
64. In **conservative** type of replication **two new strand** will be produced.
65. Both original or new strand are produced in **dispersive type** of replication.
66. Synthesize of mRAN from the DNA is known as **transcription**.
67. Restriction enzyme type two is commonly used in **genetic engineering**.
68. **Shuttle vector** can be replicate in more than one organism.
69. **YAC** - yeast artificial chromosome.
70. The PCR reaction volume usually between **20 - 100 microliter**.
71. For PCR reaction the primer should have **18 - 20 nucleotides** in length and G-C content **should be 40 - 60%**.
72. The optimum mg $^{++}$ in PCR **0.5m M**.
73. The most popular technique used for gene transfer in fish is **micro injection**.
74. In northern blotting **RNA used instead of DNA**.
75. GFP extracted from the **jelly fish**.
76. The binding site for polymerase in transcription – **TATA BOX**.
77. Dot are slot blotting analysis was first developed by **kafatos**.

78. The term bio informatics was coined by **paulienhogeweg**.
79. NCBI- national centre for biotechnology information.
80. **The microarray** technology is evolved from the **southern blotting**.
81. DNA microarray is the **multiplex** technologyused in molecular biology.
82. The principle behind the micro array technique is **hybridisation between two DNA** strand.
83. Gliovictin was isolated from **marine fungus**.
84. Marine micro algae produce **cytotoxic agent**.
85. Sea anemone produce **cardiotonic** polypeptides.
86. Insecticide is developed from **nereistoxin**.
87. Lophotoxin is obtained from **gorgonians**.
88. **Polytoxin** are extremely poisonous , synthsized by marine vibrio.
89. Most oxidized form of nitrogen in nature is NO_3^- .it is non toxic to fishes
90. **Duck weed** are used to reduce the nutrients, BOD,COD.
91. Aerobic trickling filter are used for **nitrification**.
92. Anaerobic fluidised columns for **denitrification**.
93. Ammonia oxidiser – **nitrosomonas**.
94. Nitrite oxidiser – **nitrobacter**.
95. **Halotoxin** is produced by marine sponges. it contain **pyridinium salt**.
96. Mixed microbial mate contain mostly **filamentous cyanobacteria**.
97. Microbial mate rich **in nitrogen**.
98. The word probiotic was invented by **parker**.
99. Plant reactor – **taxol**.
100. The most common organism used in recombinant fermentation is **E.coli.**
101. The first major product made by recombinant organism were **insulin**.

41

Fish Genetics

1. **Genetics** is a branch of science which deals with study of **heredity variation** among related organism.
2. **UK** established the Institute of the Biotechnology.
3. **ICGEB** - international center for genetic engineering and biotechnology which has two center **India** and **Italy**.
4. When cross is made between two parents differing in two characters known as **dihybrid** cross.
5. Mendel's first law - **Law of segregation**.
6. Mendel's second law - **law of independent assortment**.
7. When F_1 cross with its parent it is known as **back cross**.
8. When F_2 cross with recessive parent is called as **test cross**.
9. Monohybrid test cross gives **1:1 phenotype**.
10. Dihybrid test cross gives **1:1:1:1 phenotype ratio**.
11. The genetics of **qualitative phenotype** is called as **Mendel's genetics**.
12. Alternate form gene is known as **allele**.
13. Albinism is controlled by simple **autosomal recessive allele**.
14. A gene or locus which masked the action of gene at another locus was termed as **epistasis**.
15. The gene or locus which was suppressed by an epistatic gene known as **hypostatic gene**.
16. A gene whose phenotypic effect is sufficiently drastic to kill the bearer is called **lethal gene**.
17. **W.S Sutton and T. Boveri** suggested that chromosomes were the physical structure. which act as a messenger of heredity.
18. The gene is a **chemical determiner**.
19. The phenomenon of multiple effect of single gene is known as **Pleiotropism**.

20. The work on fish chromosomes began with the studied of **Retziat & Katschens**.
21. Fish cytologist had been documented chromosomes in India for 125 sp.
22. In **metacentric** chromosome – centromere located at the **center** of chromosomes.
23. **Acrocentric** - centromere located at the **end** of chromosome.
24. In **salmonids**, satellite chromosomes have been reported.
25. The length of longer arm of the chromosome divided by the length of the shorter arm is known as **arm ratio**.
26. The arm ratio is always **greater than 1**.
27. IMC - **50 chromosome**.
28. Common carp and gold fish – **104 numbers**.
29. *Heteropneustes fossilis* – **56 numbers**.
30. *C. batrachus* - **50 number**.
31. *C. striatus* - **40 numbers**.
32. The sex linked inheritance in fish was first described by **Johnnes Schmidt** in guppy.
33. **Gonochorism** is the basic mode of reproduction of sexuality.
34. Protogynous – hermaphroditism **female change in to male**.
35. Protoandrous – **male change in to female**.
36. Synchronous- **serranidae**.
37. **In XO and ZO sex determination system "O"** is the symbol for number of chromosome.
38. The tendency of gene to retain together during the process of inheritance is known as **linkage**.
39. Linkage groups in fish were first detected by **Winge**.
40. Genetic distance is expressed in the units of **crossing over** or **centimorgan** (cm).
41. One cM is equal to **1% crossing over**.
42. **FISH** is a highly effective and rapid technique for use in **gene mapping**
43. Fluorescein isothyocyanate – **green colour**.
44. The phenomenon in which two homologous chromosome fail to separate is called **non - disjunction**.
45. A pair of homologous missing from the diploid set known as **Nullisomic**.

46. **Trisomic** – one extra chromosome.
47. For chemical mutation **Nitroso ethyl urea** (NEU) are used.
48. In India 44 intergeneric and inter specific hybrids have been produced.
49. **B form** is present in most DNA in the cell.
50. In **chi - square** test the probability is less than **0.05 or 5%**.
51. Monohybrid ratio-3:1, **1:2:1**, 1:1.
52. Dihybrid ratio – **9:3:3:1** or 1:1:1:1.
53. Dominant epistasis – **12:3:1**.
54. Recessive epistasis – **9:3:4**.
55. **Masculination** of fish is usually carried out by **17 alpha methyl testosterone**.
56. The aquaculture would expand to 76 million tonnes in 2030.
57. IMC contribution towards world aquaculture is 4%.
58. IMC contribution towards Indian aquaculture is 84%.
59. Over last 2 decades, Indian fisheries have grown 6.5 times.
60. A chromosome atlas of Indian fishes depicting karyotypes of 128 teleosts found in Indian waters.
61. NBFGR – National Bureau of Fish Genetic Resources.
62. FISH – Fluorescent In-Situ Hybridization.
63. In present scenario, conserved mitochondrial DNA genes such as **cytochrome b, cytochrome coxidase** are used for phylogenic and **taxonomic validation** of fish species.
64. There are **50 DNA markers** were identified.
65. SNP – Single Nucleotide Polymorphism.
66. EST – Expressed Sequence Tags.
67. Meiosis is the process of primary gametocytes develops into eggs or sperm.
68. **Manoalide** is a bioactive compound obtained from **Pacific sponge**.
69. Gene sequence – **Operon**.
70. SOFIA – **State Of Fisheries Aquaculture**.
71. Leading country in ornamental fish culture is **Singapore**.
72. Sterile fish – **Triploid fish**.
73. Number of carbon in progesterone is **21**.
74. **C banding** is the most common type of banding for fish.

75. **Reddy** et al made the first attempt of inducing polyploidy in rohu by using **colchicine**.
76. A process of adding one or more set of chromosome to the original **diploid complement is polyploidy**.
77. **Allo polyploidy** is a process of addition of set of chromosome to the **diploid hybrid genome**.
78. Sex reversal for male – **17 alpha methyl testosterone** are used.
79. Sex reversal for female – **17 Beta Estradiol** are used.
80. The process of transferring the foreign gene to the fertilized egg is known as **transgenesis**.
81. **Micro injection** is the most common method of introducing transgene in to the developing embryo.
82. **Genetic drift** is the random **change** in the gene frequency created by the **sampling error**.
83. The role of micro chromosome not fully understood it contain redundant genetic material.
84. **Crossing over** increases genetic and phenotypic variance in population.
85. The dominant gene action produce **3 genotype** and and **2 phenotype**.
86. There are **6 types** of epistasis are present.
87. Incomplete dominant gene action produce **3 genotype and 3 phenotype**.
88. **Sex limited** phenotype will express only in one sex.
89. Distance between two gene is determined by **crossing over percentage**.
90. Random change gene frequency is known as **genetic drift**.